Training
The Teenager for the Game of Their Life

Kris Gebhardt

GCI Press

Published by GCI Press
Indianapolis, IN

Printed in the United States of America.

97 98 99 00 01   10 9 8 7 6 5 4 3 2 1

Library of Congress Cataloging-in-Publication Data

Gebhardt, Kris, 1964-
    Training the teenager for the game of their life / Kris Gebhardt.
      p.   cm.
    ISBN 1-891947-00-1
    1. Physical fitness for youth. 2. Sports for youth. 3. Sports--Training. I. Title.
GV443.G34 1998   97-51404
613.7'043--dc21   CIP

The author and publisher assume no responsibility for any injury that may occur as a result of attempting to do any of the movements, techniques or exercises described in this book. This book requires strenuous physical activity and a physical examination is advisable before starting this or any other exercise program.

Table of Contents

Contributors

I wish to offer a special thanks to all who worked so hard to bring this book to press. I could not have done it without your help.

Editor
Kathy Prata

Layout and Design
Heather Lowhorn

Cover Design & Photo Scanning
Jeff Wheeler

Photography
Garry Chilluffo

Photography
Tom Padgett

Equipment Supplier
Pete Grimmer & Chris Lynch

Acknowledgements

I would like to thank all those listed below who unselfishly gave their time and energy to help me achieve my goals. Each nurture the seeds that grew into the material that you are about to read in their own special ways. They saw potential; they encouraged, pushed, pulled, and directed me...They all said, "You can!"

To a special grade school teacher...
Steve Burke, Slate Run Elementary School

Coaches, whom I could never repay...
Ron Weiglib, NAHS-FCHS (1977-1983)
Doug Hosier, New Albany High School (1979-1982)
Gary Austin, New Albany High School (1979-1982)
Jim Binkley, New Albany High School (1979-1982)
Phil Thrasher, New Albany High School (1979-1982)
Charles Coe, Ball State University (1982-1984)
Tim Kish, Ball State University (1982-1984)
Dwight Wallace, Ball State University (1982-1984)

Employers who gave me an opportunity...
Tom Minick, Sheriff of Wastenaw County, Ann Arbor, Michigan
Tom Monaghan, President and Chairman of Domino's Pizza, Inc.
Bob Block, Bob Block Sports and Fitness Corp.

Mentors who provided encouragement, direction, and support...
Tom Minick, Vice President of Domino's Pizza, Inc.
Frank Zane, Three-time Mr. Olympia

Special Friends who are always there...
Steve Hoffacker, Hoffacker Health and Fitness
Pete Grimmer, Pro Industries

Dedication

To my wonderful children, Kraig, Kristian, and Sydney...

May the principles in this book touch and govern your lives.

To my wife, Angela
Words could never express!

To my mother, father, sister, and brother
Thanks for always being there!

To my nieces and nephews — Adam, Amanda, Andrew, Blake, Conrad, Helena, Jarrod, Jessie, Jimmie, Kevin, Kristen, Max, Monica, Nichole, Pasquall, Travis, Tyler, Wesley, Zach...

You can!

Foreword
by Mike Wanchic

When Kris first asked me to write the foreword for *Training the Teenager for the Game of Their Life* I was honored and, well, a little bit embarrassed. I mean, I have a sports background and training has meant a lot in my life, but I'm not a professional athlete — I'm a musician. What qualifies me to write this foreword? But when I sat down and started to think about what fitness has meant in my life, the idea of writing this foreword started to make sense. It's not just about being an athlete, it's about how the principles of athletics can enrich every aspect of your life. It's about how the discipline learned in training can be applied to realize any dream you have.

For the last 20 years, I have traveled the world as a professional rock musician. As John Mellencamp's co-producer and band leader, I rely daily on the discipline that I developed through swimming, wrestling and playing football as an adolescent. In my career I use fitness to help deal with stress management and the rigors of the road. If you're not in shape at the beginning of an extended road tour, your not going to make it. Endurance is a big key in dealing with contentious situations, and training is a direct outlet for stress.

My early experiences with sports have greatly influenced my life. I carry them with me everyday. They were the first time I realized that consistent effort pays off. I learned that the quickest, easiest route isn't always the best route. For example, as a teenager I did everything I could to pursue excellence in sports. I went beyond the daily practice after school — I worked out alone every morning, too. The persistence and hard work paid off. I excelled as an AAU swimmer, and was MVP and all-state in both football and wrestling. Football opened the door to my college career as an athlete/scholar at DePauw University. Succeeding in sports can teach you to succeed in anything because training is not so far removed from the arts, business — whatever you want to do. It's all about discipline; putting in the necessary work for the desired results.

Last year Kris accompanied the band on the Mr. Happy Go Lucky tour. He trained with John daily as well as with other members of the group. The experience of training with Kris dramatically effected the way I work out. He is the first "body sculptor" I have ever met. And just look at him — he knows what he's doing!

Kris' approach is not what one normally thinks of when he thinks of a trainer. Kris isn't the stereotypical drill-sergeant. He is soft-spoken, subtle and positive. He concentrates on body development instead of bulk. Before I trained with Kris, I thought overtraining was the only way to improve on my body. I now know that more is not always better. Kris has taught me that in 30 minutes I can work all the major muscle groups and get amazing results.

Knowing Kris and training with him has been a big inspiration. I absolutely believe that working out with Kris has changed John Mellencamp's life for the better. John has changed his physique and his habits. Training is now an important part of his daily routine — it wasn't before. That's not surprising, though. It's hard to be around Kris and not be motivated to do your best.

And that's what I want to invite you do to. Read this book and let Kris inspire you to be your best. The body you have now is not the body you are predetermined to have tomorrow. Kris is living proof of that. Take a look at the before and after photos in this book. They are incredible! He doesn't even look like the same person. So take heart, maybe you're not the best player on the team, maybe you're not even on the team yet — with dedication you can achieve your goals.

In *Training the Teenager for the Game of their Life* Kris has done a great job of taking the complexity out of training. He has designed an array of training programs that are easy to understand and follow, and, something I really like, there are over 1000 exercise demonstration photos showing proper technique. Each sport-specific training program is set up in an easy to follow format eliminating all the guess work.

By learning and adopting Kris' training philosophy and techniques you will not only be able to get into fantastic shape and improve your sports performance, but you will also be able to gain the advantage to mentally and physically excel in every area of your life.

What else can I say? You've got all the information you need right here in your hand. Use it and get ready for the game of your life...

Mike Wanchic

A Special Note to Parents

In my life time, I have had the opportunity to experience many great things. I have succeeded on the playing field, jet-setted around the world, worked in corporate America, and started a successful small business. I traveled with Rock Star John Mellencamp and Domino's Pizza President Tom Monaghan. I've dined with Dick Vitale and professional athletes. I've met Norman Vincent Peale, trained with Mr. Olympia Frank Zane, and traveled to some of the most beautiful locations in the world.

But it all fails in comparison to the joy and jubilation I feel about producing this book.

This year my oldest son became a teenager. As he entered this new stage of his life, I began to see a young boy maturing both physically and mentally. This brought back memories. It seemed like only yesterday that I was practicing football, going to classes, or hanging out with my friends.

His life became a reflection of my own, especially as he began to notice his body. He too was a little overweight, just like I was, and this caused him to be insecure and hesitant.

Much like my story, sports and fitness offered my son a vehicle for his self-development. He joined the cross country, basketball, and soccer teams. And he began working out. Although I truly know the results that these practices bring, I was shocked at just how much this improved his self-esteem, his confidence, and at just how much his body changed. It made me very proud to be involved in this business. To see him and others grow mentally and physically as a result of my work is the greatest reward I can have.

Shopping through the bookstores, as I always do, I noticed there was nothing like this book on the shelves for young people. There are books on sports and a few on weight lifting. Adult sections contain hundreds of books on self-development, fitness, peak performance, and self-improvement. But these titles were lacking in the youth section. I thought to myself, what better stage in one's life to build the foundation of success, fitness, and peak performance than in your teen years?

So I have written this book and in it I have elaborated on my personal philosophy. I believe training and sports are perfect vehicles for self-development. My books are not simply about lifting weights, jogging, or eating right. They uniquely blend physical training, personal fitness, peak performance, and personal development. My mental and physical approach to excellence revolves around training for "self-development" -- developing the whole person in body, mind, and spirit.

I anticipate that your sons or daughters will reap many benefits from this book. They will build stronger, healthier bodies and improve their sports performances. They will also learn the secrets, principles, and practices that will make them more successful for the rest of their lives.

I have included a special chapter just for you parents, which will make your job of supporting your child or children easier. This chapter will address issues like: When it's safe for your child to begin a training program; how you can best encourage, motivate, and support your child. There are also tips on how you can get involved in this self-development program and make it fun for the whole family.

You have in your hands a book that will make the most meaningful impact not only on your sons' or daughters' bodies and health, but on their mental attitudes and the overall success they achieve in their lives. The information contained in the following chapters will provide them with the foundation, strategies, and encouragement they need to pursue personal excellence — in body, mind, and spirit.

Simply put, this book isn't just about getting into shape, or become a great athlete — it's about building a positive, successful, healthy lifestyle.

Introduction

At the age of 14, I picked up my first dumbbell. That day changed my life. Little did I know then that those early days of training and the discipline of playing team sports would become the foundation for all of the successes in my life. I never would have guessed that pressing dumbbells, running laps around the track, and hours and hours of practice after classes would prepare me for the jobs that I've worked or even starting my own business. But it did.

Training for sports and conditioning my body taught me all the important lessons everyone needs to be a success. I discovered how to set and achieve goals, develop my motivation, pursue my dreams, and become dedicated by practicing hard and consistently. I also learned how to give 100 percent of myself to my training, as well as to deal with setbacks and adversity.

Teenagers are always faced with challenges and choices. When I was growing up, many of my classmates were "hanging out," experimenting with drugs, and getting into trouble. But my friends and I chose a different way to spend our time. We hit the gym, and it became an awesome training ground for many of our successes.

Today, your challenges are even more demanding. However, you too can choose a positive way to use your time and energy and build a foundation for your positive future.

I know you can because I've been there. And it hasn't always been easy, and I haven't always been in shape. As a teen I was overweight and troubled with knee injuries. I was also teased by my classmates because of my weight. (I wasn't a gifted athlete and had to work hard to develop my skills.)

It would have been easy to fall into the drug scene or just throw in the towel and hang out. But instead, I began training my body and my mind. This book shares the secrets of how to get into the best possible shape — physically and mentally. And by doing so create a life that many believe to be impossible.

Training the Teenager for the Game of Their Life will teach you: how to take control of your body and your life; how to train for self-development in personal fitness and sports; how to train mentally to become a peak performer and a better winner; how to apply the lessons that you learn on the field, on the court, or in the weight room to all other areas of your life. You'll learn tips for your general health, sports, and your life.

Topics covered for General Health include:
- Losing Weight
- Gaining Weight
- Toning, defining, and building your muscles
- Developing strength
- Eating for good health
- Training at home, the club, or the school gym

For Sports, we'll talk about:
- Training specifically for your sport
- Training in the off-season, pre-season, and post-season
- Increasing your stamina, speed, and endurance
- Becoming more agile and flexible
- Rehabilitation for injuries
- Eating for competition and training
- Training without drugs

And for those other areas of Life, there are tips on:
+ Learning the importance of building good relationships
+ Training your brain with brain-building exercises
+ Developing a winners mind-set
+ Mentally preparing for training and the big game
+ Talking to yourself (no it doesn't mean you're crazy)
+ Adopting a positive attitude
+ Setting and achieving your goals
+ Modeling the success of others
+ How to change
+ How to pursue your dreams
+ Plus much, much more

When you buy a stereo, computer, bicycle, or car, they all come with an owner's manual. But when you were born, you weren't given an owner's manual. This is the owner's manual you were never given for your body and your mind.

This "manual" will give you straightforward information on becoming a peak performer — on and off the playing field. There will be no sugar-coated promises; nor will it paint pictures of unrealistic expectations, or claim its "easy-street."

Practice, determination, dedication, persistence, and effort are the universal ingredients to achieving all worthy goals — whether it be to build your biceps, ace that chemistry exam, or be an outstanding ball player. There are no short-cuts. There never has been, nor will there ever be. There are no miracle diets, shakes, pills or workouts. You must be prepared to do the work and put in the effort. And if you do, the rewards will be unlimited. You will create a life that will match your most wildest dreams.

Training the Teenager for the Game of Their Life

Seventeen years old. It's been a long week. Hard practices and two tests. Tomorrow is the big game. Scouts from Kentucky, University of Louisville, and Western Kentucky will be there to watch. The pressure is on. I've been training for eight years. Got to get that scholarship. No scholarship, no college.

This is a great pre-game party. Everyone needs it. Tension's been high. A lot of the guys are getting really wasted. Tim has had six beers. A beer sure sounds good. But I better not give into the pressure. Got to focus on the game tomorrow. Can't screw up. Can't throw it all away to fit in with the crowd. Better go home early and go to bed. Need my rest.

• • •

Ten Years Later
It's been a hard week. Trying to pay off the bills. The kids have been sick with the flu. Thank God it's Friday. This is a great party. The guys from the office are really drinking a lot. Jon keeps pushing beers

on me. Can't drink. Tomorrow's the big interview. Got to get that job. It's a dream job. Can't screw it up by drinking all night. Better go home and get some sleep. I need my rest.

• • •

The decisions you make today, will affect the rest of your life. The way you approach the game and practice for the game reflect how you'll approach the challenges you'll have later in your life.

Do you see the parallel? Nobody could have convinced me at age 16 that the decisions I made nor the discipline I followed would have had such an impact later in my life.

Training the Teenager for the Game of Their Life is an exciting book. It will change your life.

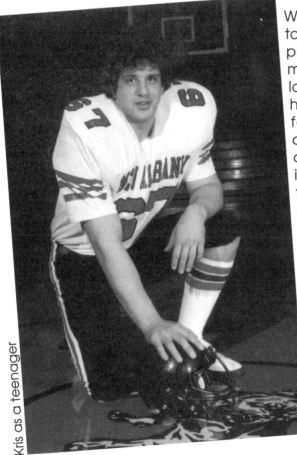

Kris as a teenager

Whether you picked up this book to be healthier, get into shape, supercharge your sports performance, or learn the secrets of lifelong success, you have in your hands a resource of valuable information that will help you achieve degrees of success that are greater than you could ever imagine. You will learn the secrets that will help you become a winner with your health, on the playing field, and in life.

The forty-three chapters in this book are a blueprint for immediate success, as well as for your future success. Each chapter draws on a variety of proven principles of philosophy, business, personal development, physical training, and sports performance, and used by some of the greatest athletes, business people, and leaders in today's world. With this encyclopedia of information, you'll get into great shape, supercharge your sports performance, and become a winner for the rest of your life.

As a teenager, I had the unique experience of being exposed to these principles and success ideas. Throughout my life I have been able to apply these ideas and principles to walk on and earn a scholarship as a Division I football player, land a dream job working as an assistant to the president of a Fortune 500 company, write and produce four books, and own and operate two businesses. How?

Because "Everything that I ever needed to learn about success in life I learned on the playing field and in the weight room."

The Biggest Mistake That I Have Ever Made

The day my athletic career ended, I quit being an athlete. I quit training. I became an average person. I was no longer a champion. I got an average job and became a washed-up, 250 pound, overweight ex-jock. My days lost meaning. I got up, went to work, and earned a paycheck and fell into the daily grind.

I threw away all the lessons I learned as an athlete. I tossed aside my dreams, my dedication, perseverance, hard work, and the desire to sweat. After all, who needs to be in shape to work nine to five?

Yet my life seemed empty. I was going nowhere. I thought I didn't have to exercise anymore since I wasn't playing a sport.

I forgot how to be a winner and all the valuable lessons I learned as an athlete and the skills I learned in training.

That was twelve years ago. Today it's different.

How did I turn my life around? I went back to being an athlete.

An Athlete Forever!

I got recommitted. I started dreaming again, like I did as a high school athlete when I dreamt of playing Division One football. I began to set goals, just like the ones I used to graduate from school. I began to think of myself as an athlete in the sport of life.

I began a physical training program that would get me in the very best shape. I had learned many times on the playing field that an in shape body performs the best. I began to view life as the big game! I began to surround myself with people who were winners. And I set out to become a champion. What I realized was that life was a sport...the big game...the ultimate season. In order to succeed, I had to train like a champion. The requirements to succeed in life are the same as for sports — sacrifice, hard work, training, dedication, perseverance, and commitment.

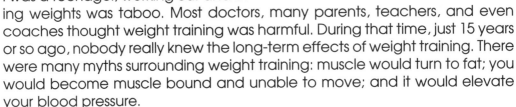

Today It's Different

You're fortunate today to be living in a time when society supports the notion of fitness and good health. It might be hard to imagine, but when I was a teenager, working out and lifting weights was taboo. Most doctors, many parents, teachers, and even coaches thought weight training was harmful. During that time, just 15 years or so ago, nobody really knew the long-term effects of weight training. There were many myths surrounding weight training: muscle would turn to fat; you would become muscle bound and unable to move; and it would elevate your blood pressure.

Fortunately none of this is true. Yet at that time, several of my buddies and I had to hide our weight training workouts from our coaches. As a matter of fact, my high school didn't have a weight room. My friends and I trained in a garage heated by a wood burning stove on homemade equipment.

There were stereotypes as well associated with weight training. Back then only stupid people or block heads lifted weights. How wrong those ideas were. Today, it's the intelligent people that participate in weight training. People who spend time keeping their bodies in shape know that their success outside the gym is determined by the amount of effort, perseverance, dedication, and sweat that they invest lifting weights, running on the treadmill, riding the stationary bike, and even visualizing their goals of a fit, healthy body.

Training the Teenager for the Game of Their Life

This is the book all adults wish they had when they were growing up. It's a handbook for success for anything you choose to do in your life.

This is a three part book. In **Part One** — General Fitness Training — I will discuss all the important elements for general fitness. Included are chapters on aerobic training, weight training, nutrition, shape training for teenage girls, training for "safe" weight loss and "safe" weight gain, as well as special exercises for preteens. This part is loaded with valuable information, training techniques, photos of each exercise, and much more.

Part Two is dedicated to training for sports. There are specific training programs for twelve of the most popular sports —football, hockey, baseball, basketball, track, golf, gymnastics, soccer, wrestling, cross country, tennis, extreme sports, and volleyball. Each of these chapters contains pre-season, post-season, and in-season training programs with specific exercises for each sport demonstrated with photos.

Also in Part Two is a chapter on training for speed improvement, stretching and flexibility, overtraining and injuries, the importance of supplements, training at school or the gym, home gym training, drug-free training, and developing good player-coach and player-player relationships.

Part Three is my favorite part of the book. It is dedicated to strengthening your mind. It includes chapters on developing a winner's mind-set; mentally preparing for training and sports; what to say when you talk to yourself; becoming a peak performer; attitude is everything; setting goals; developing mental toughness; finding models and mentors; really good advice for parents; and the real rewards of training and sports. These chapters are mental exercises designed to strengthen and tone your mental abilities.

All chapters are short and to the point. You won't have to waste time sorting through a bunch of scientific mumbo jumbo. Each is complete so you can easily refer back to just what you want, anytime you like.

Kris as a teenager

Kris today as author

Conclusion

I didn't know at age fourteen when I first picked up a dumbbell that I would be conducting an experiment with my own body on the long-term effects of training, fitness, weight training, aerobic exercise, and good nutritional practices.

I cannot imagine what would have happened if I had not been exposed to these important practices. They have had such a positive impact on my life. They have given me the skills I needed to overcome some pretty rough times and some fairly large obstacles — all of which were overshadowed with a lot of frustration, fear, and anxiety.

There are many reasons you might want to become involved in a personal fitness program. You could take up weight training, aerobic exercise, and good nutritional practices to look better, to be healthier, to be a better ball player, or to get stronger. The list could go on. . .

But I believe it's best to adopt the philosophy of training for "Self-Development" — training to become the best you can be all around. Training for self-development — to become a better person — is an approach which will catapult you far beyond the sixteen-inch biceps or a record bench press. You will become conditioned to be a champion in life.

Training for self-development blends personal fitness and physical training with mental and emotional development. The goal is always is to develop the whole person — body, mind, and soul. And this is done by training the mind as well as the body. Where the mind goes, the body will follow. Think about what that will do for your game, for your life!

The picture you see on the cover of this book is the result of living by these principles. The results have been not only a super, in-shape, well-conditioned body and a clear focused mind, but a fit career, family, and social life.

You can use this approach to personal fitness and sports to get yourself and your life in tip-top shape and keep it there forever!

What is a Training Program?

Webster's Dictionary defines "training" as a means to instruct or condition to some manner of behavior or performance. "Program" is described as the organized effort to achieve a goal by stages or a set of logical steps to solve a problem.

So your training program could be thought of as an organized effort of logical steps of instruction and conditioning that will help you to produce the behavior, performance, and results that you seek.

A successful training program must have a well-developed plan, centered around activities and exercises that are conducive to the ultimate goal. So just as an Olympic athlete needs to develop a training program to get into the best shape possible to compete in this top world event, so too must you develop a program that will sharpen your skills to reach your goals — whatever they may be.

Careful attention must be given to the formulation of your training program. It's not just an exercise, a mindless activity, or pure recreation.

A good training program should be thought of as self-development — activities that sharpen your skills to become the best you can be.

Training Is a Time for Discovery
In training you will learn much about yourself. You will go beyond your former boundaries, face challenges, overcome fears, and weaknesses, and, at the same time, build new strengths. Your training program will stimulate positive feelings and emotions — the fuel you need to actively pursue all of your goals.

There are many secrets to formulating a successful training program. The first is that it is unique to you. Your training program is yours. Don't expect to train in exactly the same way as your friends.

Developing your training program is going to involve your efforts. It requires self-study, personal assessment, and careful calculation, as well as commitment, persistence, and consistency.

Once you've decided that you are going to start a training program, you will need to put together an action plan — a system or an organized way of accomplishing your goals. It will require a series of practices or training sessions, grouped together and practiced consistently in order for you to obtain the results you desire.

And notice throughout this book I use the word "train" or "training." To me training stimulates positive physical and mental growth. A "workout" implies drudgery and is usually something not engaged in with enthusiasm. So every time you start to say to your friends "I gotta go workout or to practice" with a long sigh — stop yourself and switch your choice of words and your tone to reflect enthusiasm. "I'm going to go train!"

There's a universal law that states what you sow, so shall you reap. This literally means that you get back exactly what you put out. For instance, if you approach your training sessions with enthusiasm, you will gain energy. If you approach your training sessions with dread and a feeling that you "should" go "workout," you will very likely leave the gym feeling depleted of energy.

The Structure of Your Training Program

There are many different ways to train, as well as many different opinions and theories on what makes a good training program. So it's very easy to get frustrated, confused, and misled.

Each month magazines like *Muscle and Fitness*, *Men's Health*, and *Shape* present different training programs and exercise which very often leave the reader wondering which way is right. It's important to remember that there are many different ways and reasons to train, and that no one way is right over another. It depends on your goals and your activities. For instance a volleyball player might train one way, a football player another. A body-builder trains differently than a powerlifter.

Some experts are going to tell you to lift weights three times a week, other twice a week. Some are going to tell you to eat a high carbohydrate diet; others will tell you to keep your carbohydrate intake low.

There is really no one right way to train. The only "right way" is the one that works for you and one that you feel comfortable with. The way you determine which way is right for you is to experiment and try different routines and exercises, then judge the results. This is done by listening to your inner voice. You tap into how your body feels and responds to a particular training program. You need to judge it by the results you get. Then you need to change it if it just doesn't feel right or it's not working. Leave it if it does. Your body ultimately knows best.

There are five very important factors that need to be considered in every training program:

1. Personal Training Philosophy
2. Individual Characteristics
3. Goals
4. Lifestyle
5. Specific Needs

Your Personal Training Philosophy could be defined as your current and evolving beliefs about training in general. It's your basic theory of training. As I wrote in Chapter One, my personal training philosophy centers around training for "self-development." Again, that means not only training to get into shape, or to improve athletic skills, but to become a better person all the way around — a peak performer on and off the field. This means that I am not only training to get into fantastic shape, but I am training to become a better author, father, employer, husband, and citizen. To me this is a good philosophy because it extends your motivation and drive to continue training outside of your immediate goals. Those that adopt this philosophy will continue to train forever as long as the desire to improve themselves remains. Those that don't usually stop training when the season ends.

Another very important factor relating to the success of your training program is your Individual Characteristics. As human beings we were all created differently. You are unique. No two people are exactly the same. So it makes sense that if we are different then no one generic training program is going to work best for each of us. The best training program is the one that has been custom molded to fit your individual characteristics and needs. This is accomplished by taking an inventory of your personal characteristics and personal situations. However, this is not as hard as it sounds. You can simply begin with a generic training program and as you experiment with it you can adjust it to fit your needs. A generic exercise program can't take into consideration your personal characteristics, individual ability, goals, level of experience, motivation, or resources.

Physical and Mental Considerations
When designing your training program, there are several important factors to take into consideration.

1. Body Type
It is extremely important to get an idea of your body type in order to ensure that you are participating in the correct type of workout that will provide you with the best results. When I set up a training program for a client, I take their body type into consideration. If they are short and stocky, I know that they will most likely find it relatively easy to put on muscle mass. So I will recommend that they do a variety of basic movements but also a variety of shaping movements. This allows them to develop proportionately, well-shaped muscles instead of just thick bulky ones. I move them through their workouts with the least amount of rest time between sets and reps, and I will pay close attention to their diet.

The key is to recognize your body type and then apply the right training program. Learning and understanding your body type can save you a lot of wasted time and frustration. Although certain principles of training are the same for all body types, the way in which you set up your program and the techniques you adopt can make a profound difference depending on what type of body you were given at birth.

You can even change your body type to some degree. Look at the pictures below. In the picture on the left, weighing 250 pounds, I look very large and bulky. On the right, I now look streamlined, well-defined, and in shape.

As a developing teenager, your body will be changing a lot. My best advice is to continue with the programs outlined in this book and make adjustments as you feel the need. By discovering your body type and applying these training programs for your body, you could achieve fantastic results.

2. Current Level of Fitness

Your current level of fitness is a critical element you must consider when designing your program. I frequently see people get their ambitions smashed by setting their sights too high and going at it too hard and too quickly, especially when they are terribly out of shape. This usually results in burnout, injury, and loss of motivation to train. What is your current condition?

3. Training Experience

Your training experience is a very important factor of consideration; however, it is not a limiting factor. How much training experience do you have? More times than not, clients who come to me with no prior experience wind up being the most successful. So don't fret over lack of experience. Remember this — when I first started weight training, I didn't even know the difference between a dumbbell and a weight machine.

4. Goals and Objectives

You need to be able to define and have a clear understanding of your goals and objectives. Goals are the "what" you want to accomplish. You will need to spend some time seriously thinking about what you really want to accomplish in your training program. And you need to be more specific than just saying you want to start to exercise or to become a better athlete. Your goals need to be more clear and more specific, such as "I want to gain ten pounds of muscle." Or, "I want to decrease my forty yard dash time by one tenth."

At first, you may have a hard time identifying your specific goals, but with practice it will become easier and your goals will become more clear.

5. Physical Energy

How much "fuel" do you have to dedicate to your training? All of us have different energy levels. Some have high levels, some low. There are many things that affect your energy level. In the following chapters you will learn how to increase your energy as well as how to avoid things that zap your energy. Remember: Everything in life requires energy — whether you strive to be a good student, a good employee, or a good athlete. Energy production will be very important to you, both now and in the future.

6. Motivation Level

Your motivation level is as unique as your body type. All of us are motivated differently and at different levels or degrees. Obviously someone with a higher level of motivation is going to need a more stimulating training program. It's important that you match your training program appropriately to your level of motivation. If not you'll have a mismatch that will create varying degrees of frustration and a lack of interest. You will need to continually work to develop your motivation. It's not something that we are born with.

Other Important Keys

Balance and good decision making are also important factors to a successful training program. Training should not throw your life out of balance. It should fit into your lifestyle relatively comfortably. While there may be some sacrifices to make, some bad habits to shed, your training program should enhance your life.

An unbalanced approach to training always leads to burnout, fatigue, and overtraining. Many people jump into a training program full of enthusiasm, adopting a more is better attitude. While they may achieve some quick results, as times goes on very few of these people continue training at all.

Remember the tale of the tortoise and the hare — Slow and steady wins the race.

There are many important decisions you need to make before beginning your training program, as well as many decision you will need to make as you progress through your training. All decisions are important, regardless of their size and magnitude. You need to ask yourself:

- Where am I going to train — at school, the club, home?
- What type of training program do I want to use?
- When am I going to train?
- Am I going to need a training partner?

♦ Do you need a trainer or a coach?
♦ Can I obtain the information I need through books, tapes, and videos?

These are important considerations. I've seen many people make crucial mistakes with the decisions they make like picking the wrong place to train or not getting the proper instruction.

The Complete Training Program

In order for a training program to be totally effective, it should be complete. A complete training program should center around six key areas:

♦ Mental Training Exercises
♦ Aerobic (Cardiovascular) Exercises
♦ Weight Training Exercises
♦ Good Nutrition Practices
♦ Attention to Recovery
♦ A System of Checks and Balances

Mental Training

Mental training is what I refer to as "brain building." These are mental exercises like goal setting, visualization, and self-talk. These exercise are designed to strengthen, tone, and develop your intellectual muscles. Successful training is not just the result of physical activity. Where the mind goes the body will follow. In Part III, I will introduce you to many brain-building exercises that will help you train more focused, as well as increase your motivation, desire, and ambition.

Aerobic (Cardiovascular) Exercise

Proper conditioning of the cardiovascular system (heart, lungs, circulatory system) is important in your overall health and well-being. It is a vital ingredient to get your body in tip-top shape and in good working order.

There are a wide range of exercises, activities, and routines designed to develop and condition your cardiovascular system. These include walking, jogging, running, stair climbing, stationary biking, rowing, cross-country skiing, aerobic classes, and weight training. Many competitive sports such as basketball and soccer are also avenues to revving up your cardiovascular system.

Remember, you will have unique cardiovascular training needs. Training intensity, routines, and activities will ultimately be determined by your goals and current fitness level.

Chapter four will give you in-depth instruction on how to develop your own aerobic training program. Further instruction for specific sports will be addressed in Part II.

Weight Training

Weight training or resistance training is by far the best and most practical way to strengthen, tone, shape, and mold body muscles. For the purposes of this book, resistance training centers around weight training exercises: free weights (dumbbells and barbells) and weight machines.

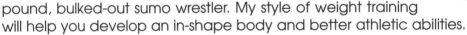

The goals of weight training are to increase and maintain strength, develop muscle mass, shape, tone, and increase muscular endurance. Adopting the style of weight training that I am teaching will not make you a 300-pound, bulked-out sumo wrestler. My style of weight training will help you develop an in-shape body and better athletic abilities.

In the chapters that follow, you will be given advice on how to design your program at different training levels. There will be information on weight training for general fitness, as well as training for different sports. Stretching, lifting techniques, sets, reps, and cool-downs will also be discussed.

And before you can effectively use weights to mold and shape your muscles, you must know where to look for the muscles. I have included basic anatomy illustrations in the Chapter Three. However, with over 600 muscles in the body, you can be sure that I'm not going to discuss every muscle. I'll give you just the information that you need to be a success with your training.

Nutrition

Good nutritional practices will probably determine between 60 and 80 percent of your overall training success. This area is often neglected and overlooked by athletes and people who train for general fitness.

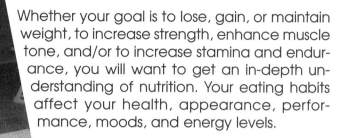

Whether your goal is to lose, gain, or maintain weight, to increase strength, enhance muscle tone, and/or to increase stamina and endurance, you will want to get an in-depth understanding of nutrition. Your eating habits affect your health, appearance, performance, moods, and energy levels.

In Chapter Seven, we examine important nutritional topics such as when to eat, what to eat, why to eat, and how to eat. We'll look at supplements, suggested foods, meal schedules, food journals, shortcuts, as well as secrets and tips for maintaining good nutritional practices. To provide your body with the nutrients it needs to grow and develop, perform at its best, and recover from training and everyday stresses means eating the right combination of foods along with adopting a good supplementation program.

This doesn't mean, you will never be able to eat out again. You'll still be able to hang out with your friends at the mall. You may, however, find yourself choosing energy producing foods, while your friends opt for energy draining greasy fries and burgers.

Recovery

Like nutrition, too often the recovery stage of a training program is overlooked and seldom discussed. But recovery is just as important as the actual training session.

Because of the mental and physical demands of training, it's very important to place special importance on recovery. In weight training, the muscles do not increase in size (hypertrophy) until after they have thoroughly recovered from your preceding workout. Muscles grow during the resting phase of training, not during the actual lifting. I have a training equation that I follow:

Intelligent Training + Nutrition + Rest = Results

Physical training is an important part of your program, but overtraining is often the cause of failure. Training too hard, too long, and too often — without the proper attention to recovery — is going to diminish the results you get, and perhaps even set you up for injury and burnout.

Intelligent training means getting the most from the least amount of effort. You must train with intensity and focus. Merely going through the motions will get you nowhere. And you must eat nutritious foods for your body to recover.

Rest is also a vital part of the recovery process. We all know that the body requires rest to perform at its best. This includes adequate sleep and enough relaxation time during our waking hours to bring about a state of physical and mental refreshment. This too is individualized. Some people can get by with seven or eight hours sleep, others need ten or twelve.

Training places many demands on you physically and mentally. In order to be successful with your program you need to figure into your training schedule: time off, sleep, recreation, stress managements, rest periods, and layoffs.

In the following chapters, I make recommendations for your training program that will include attention to recovery. Take these seriously.

System of checks and balances
It's pretty hard to stick to something if the effort you are investing isn't giving you a payoff, or you don't feel like you're making any progress.

Academically, tests provide the feedback you need to know whether all those hours spent with your nose in your books is paying off. It seems to work the same with training.

It is extremely important that you set up a system of checks and balances to keep track of your progress. It is essential that you give yourself this kind of feedback, because if you don't you will be less likely to stick with the program.

Checks and balances fall into two categories — informal and scientific.

For general fitness most people rely on the informal methods to gauge their progress. These include: photographs, videotaping, tape measures, and scales. They're easy to use and require little time and effort.

If you're training for sports, you may find that your coaches and trainers rely on more scientific methods for testing your body's response to your training program. These include: muscular fitness tests, cardiovascular fitness tests, and body composition analysis. These offer a more precise, scientific measurement of your progress and seem to appeal to people who are more statistically minded and like cold, hard facts.

Your training program should become a very special part of your life. For the best results view it as a lifelong commitment to self-development, growth, and advancement in all areas of your life. A training session should be thought of as a chapter in the book of your life. It's not just a workout. It's a sacred time that you invest today to make yourself better in the future. There's no question that physical fitness affects your total well-being. It spills over directly into your social life, your sports performance, your grades — every nook and cranny of your existence. Treat your training program — and in essence your body — with the importance and respect that it deserves.

Part 1

Training Programs for General Fitness

3 The Teenager's Body

The wonder machine

Have you ever really thought about all the things your body does in a 24-hour period? It can be mind-boggling. Your body has over hundreds of intricately devised cells, muscles, and bones (not to mention the organs), which synchronistically work together to get you through your day. And the best thing about your body and its functions is that you don't have to think about it at all — that is, unless you want it to perform even better.

The Parts of the Human Machine

Getting started on a training program requires that you learn about your body. Specifically, we are concerned with two things

- The muscles of the body — how they work, where they are, and what they do.
- Your cardiovascular system (heart, lungs, and circulatory system), how it works, what its function is during exercise.

However, in the first stages of training, it is not necessary that you dissect a cadaver and study and memorize all of the over 600 muscles in the body. In fact, you really don't have to know more than the basic muscle groups and be able to locate them on your body. As you advance with your training, you will want to increase your knowledge further and learn more.

The Muscles of the Machine
For our purposes, the body can be divided into six groups: chest, back, shoulders, arms, midsection, and lower body.

The chest
The pectoral consists of two parts — the *clavicular* (upper) portion and the *sternal* (lower) portion. The upper part is attached to the clavicle (collarbone). Along the mid body line, it attaches to the sternum (breastbone) and to the cartilage of several ribs. The largest mass of the pectoral starts at the upper arm bone (humerus), and is fastened at a point under and just above where the deltoids attach to the humerus. The pectorals spread out like a fan and cover the rib cage like armor plates.

Attached to the rib cage in the center and across to the shoulder, this muscle lets you perform such motions as pitching a ball underhanded, doing a wide arm bench press, or twisting a cap off a bottle.

The back
The flat triangular muscle that extends out and down from the neck and down between the shoulder blades is the *trapezius*. The primary function of the trapezius is to raise the shoulder girdle.

The *Latissimus dorsi* (Lats) are the large triangular muscles that extend from under the shoulders down to the small of the back on both sides. Their primary function is to pull the shoulders downward.

The *Spinal erectors*, composed of several muscles in the lower back that guard the nerve channels, work to hold the spine erect, straighten the spine from a position with the torso flexed completely forward, and help to arch the lower and middle back.

The shoulder
The deltoids are versatile muscles that move the arm forward, backward, to the side, up, and around. The deltoids have three distinct lobes of muscle called "heads" that enable this movement: the *anterior head* (the muscle in the front), the *medial head* (the muscle on the side), and the *posterior head* (the muscle in the rear).

The arms

Biceps. The bicep (biceps brachii) is a two-headed muscle with its point of origin under the deltoid and its point of insertion below the elbow. There are two muscle groups located at the front of the upper arm that contract to flex the arm fully from a straight position. The smallest of these muscles is called the brachialis, a thin band of muscle between the biceps and triceps. The brachialis muscle runs only about halfway up the humerus bone above the elbow.

The biceps are much larger in mass than the brachialis muscles and are the primary muscle group responsible for bending the arm. With an origin near the shoulder joint and insertions on the forearm bones, the biceps bend the arm from a straight position. The secondary function of the biceps is to supinate the hand. The biceps make up about thirty-five percent of the arm mass.

Triceps. The tricep (triceps brachii), a three-headed muscle that attaches under the deltoid and below the elbow, works in opposition to the biceps to straighten the arm and supinate (twist upward) the wrist. The triceps are larger than the biceps and make up about three-quarters of the upper arm.

Forearms. The forearm is composed of a variety of muscles on the outside and inside of the lower arm that control the actions of the hand and wrist. The forearm flexor muscles curl the palm down and forward; the forearm extensor muscles curl the knuckles back and up.

The midsection

Abdomen. The visual center of the body — the abdomen — is composed of the rectus abdominis, the external obliques, and the intercostals. The abdominals have a relatively simple function. They pull your upper body (rib cage) and lower body (pelvis) toward each other, and they contribute to keeping your internal organs in place.

The rectus abdominis is a long muscle extending along the length of the ventral aspect of the abdomen. This muscle originates in the area of the pubis and inserts into the cartilage of the fifth, sixth, and seventh ribs. The basic function of the rectus abdominis is to flex the spinal column and draw the sternum toward the pelvis.

The external obliques (obliques externus abdominis) are the muscles at each side of the torso (commonly referred to as the handles). They are attached to the lower eight ribs and insert at the sides of the pelvis. The basic function of the external obliques is to flex and rotate the spinal column.

The <u>intercostals</u> are two thin planes of muscular and tendon fibers occupying the spaces between the ribs. The intercoastals lift the ribs and draw them together.

The lower body

The lower body is made up of more than 200 muscles. The majority of these muscles are located in the thighs, hips, and buttocks. Rather than trying to explain the development of every one of these muscles, we will focus on the development of the legs and buttocks. We'll also examine the main muscle groups and the function in each one.

<u>Buttocks</u>. The primary muscles of the buttocks are the *gluteus maximus* and the *gluteus medius*. The gluteus maximus contracts to help straighten the legs and torso from a completely or partially flexed position.

<u>Thighs</u>. The thigh muscles are among the largest in the human body. The main thigh muscles are the quadricepts and the hamstrings.

<u>Quadriceps</u>. The quads contract to straighten the leg from a fully or partially bent position. The quadriceps are composed of four muscles at the front of the thigh — *rectus femoris, vastus intermedius, vastus medialis*, and *vastus lateralis*.

<u>Hamstrings</u>. The primary muscle group at the back of the thigh is the biceps femoris, often called the leg biceps. This muscle group contracts to bend the leg fully from a straight or partially bent position.

<u>The Calves</u>. The primary muscles of the calf are the *soleus, gastrocnemius*, and the *tibialis anterior*. The soleus is the larger and deeper of the calf muscles and originates from both the fibula and the tibia. Its basic function is to flex the foot. The gastrocnemius has two heads, one originating from the lateral aspect and the other from the medial of the lower femur. Both heads join to overlay the soleus and join with and insert into the Achilles tendon which inserts into the heel bone. The basic function of the gastrocnemius is to flex the foot. The tibialis anterior runs up the front of the lower leg alongside the shinbone. Its basic function is to flex the foot.

The Cardiovascular/Aerobic Parts of the Human Machine

Science tells us the primary function of the cardiovascular system is to deliver blood to active tissues. This includes the delivery of oxygen and nutrients and the removal of metabolic waste products. During prolonged bouts of exercise your cardiovascular system also maintains your body temperature so you won't over heat. The cardiovascular system is composed of lungs, blood vessels, heart, arteries, capillaries, and veins.

Knowledge Equals Power

Being successful with any training program is going to require that you learn the basic anatomy outlined in this chapter. Knowing what the muscles do, where they are located, and their primary function during training is necessary to correctly follow and apply any general or sports specific training program.

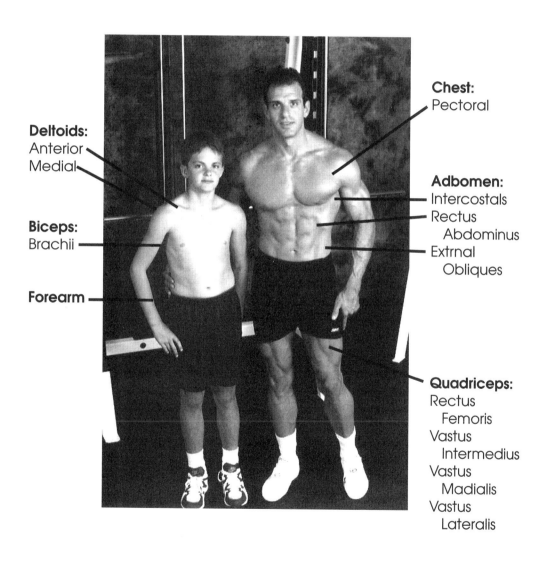

Deltoids:
Anterior
Medial

Biceps:
Brachii

Forearm

Chest:
Pectoral

Adbomen:
Intercostals
Rectus
    Abdominus
Extrnal
    Obliques

Quadriceps:
Rectus
    Femoris
Vastus
    Intermedius
Vastus
    Madialis
Vastus
    Lateralis

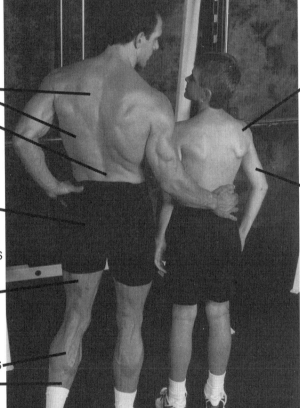

Back:
Trapezius
Latissimus Dorsi
Spinal Erectors

Buttocks:
Gluteus
   Maximus
Gluteus Medius

Hamstring:
Leg Biceps

Calves:
Gastrocnemius
Soleus

Deltoids:
Posterior

Triceps:
Brachii

Aerobic Training for General Fitness

If you want to get into great shape, control your weight, improve your athletic performance, and become fit and healthy, then you will want to include cardiovascular exercise in your training program.

A Quick Lesson in Cardiovascular Training
Cardiovascular training conditions the heart, lungs, and circulatory system. It also helps to control body weight. Your heart is the most important muscle in your body. It is a muscular pump, about the size of your fist, that beats nonstop every minute of your life, sending about 2,000 gallons of blood through your body every day.

If you want to create a strong, healthy and in-shape body, that can perform at its best, you must not neglect your cardiovascular training. Looking great on the outside means little if your heart and lungs are not functioning properly on the inside. Exercises that force you to elevate your heart rate are referred to as aerobic exercise because they allow you to breath at a steady, continuous pace as you perform them. Walking, jogging, stair climbing, treadmilling, stationary biking, rowing, cross-country skiing, doing aerobics, and many competitive sports all exercise the cardiovascular system.

Your Cardiovascular System

Science tells us that the major function of the cardiovascular system during exercise is to deliver blood to active tissues. This includes the delivery of oxygen and nutrients and the removal of the metabolic waste products. If you exercise long enough, your cardiovascular system will also maintain your body temperature so that you won't overheat.

You use your cardiovascular system in both aerobic and anaerobic exercise. Aerobic literally means "with oxygen."

Anaerobic activities use the large muscle groups, but at high intensities that exceed the body's capacity to use oxygen to supply energy. This creates an oxygen deficit by using energy produced without oxygen. Anaerobic exercise (weight lifting) eventually builds up enough of an oxygen deficit to force the exerciser to terminate the exercise session quickly. That is why you eventually run out of gas and have to stop when lifting weights.

For any training program to be complete, you should consider three primary goals for exercising the cardiovascular system.

1. Increase the capacity of the cardiovascular system (build it up).
2. Use the cardiovascular system to prolong periods of exercise in order to promote fat burning if you're trying to maintain weight or lose weight.
3. Help in developing muscle mass, strength, muscle toning, and muscular endurance and recovery.

Your number one goal of cardiovascular exercise should be to condition the cardiovascular system. You want to increase the capacity of your respiratory system — the lungs and blood vessels — and your circulatory system — heart, arteries, capillaries, and veins — in order to supply oxygen and nutrients to your muscles cells so that you can sustain physical activity for at least thirty continuous minutes. This is the minimum amount of time scientists tell us we need to exercise in order to maintain cardiovascular fitness.

Finding Your Target

You will need to focus on aerobic activities and exercise that permit you to get into the aerobic "Training Zone," sometimes called the "Target Zone."

These exercises, although strenuous, are rhythmic, and performed in a range of intensity that allows you to safely elevate your heart rate for cardiovascular benefit. You can accomplish this by walking, jogging, or using the treadmill. I like to use a heart monitor to check my heart rate and to see if I'm in the proper range for my training program.

The Aerobic Training Zone is estimated to be between 60 and 85 percent of your maximum heart rate. If you're a beginner, simply subtract your age from 220, then multiply by 60 percent. If you are at an intermediate fitness level, subtract your age from 220 and multiply by 70 percent. If you're at an advance level, subtract your age from 220 and multiply by 85 percent. The figure you arrive at represents the number of times your heart needs to beat per minute to derive the most cardiovascular benefit.

To reach the aerobic training zone, you need to engage in an aerobic workout consisting of a five to ten minute warm-up, followed by twenty minutes of aerobic training, and ending with a five to ten minute cool down. The warm-up increases your heart rate gradually, which prepares your muscular and circulatory systems for the upcoming training period. A good warm-up also helps prevent injuries to muscles, ligaments, and joints. The training period should last twenty to thirty minutes to keep your heart rate elevated in your training zone. The cool down allows your muscular and circulatory system to return to normal levels. A proper cool down will help to prevent dizziness, faintness, or nausea. It's important to train your cardiovascular system three times a week with no more than two days between training sessions to achieve a reasonable cardiovascular fitness level.

The Fat Burning Training Zone

Training at a lower intensity for longer periods of time has proven to be an effective way to burn body fat.

You can enhance the burning of unwanted body fat by lowering the intensity of aerobic exercise to the 50 to 65 percent range of your maximum heart rate, and extending the time and frequency of your training sessions. Exercises should be of moderate intensity, like slow jogging.

You can compute your Fat Burning Training Zone by using the same formula for the aerobic training zone. The training routine is also similar. It should consist of a five to ten minute warm-up, followed by 45 to 60 minutes of low intensity exercise, and end with five to ten minutes of cool down. You should also increase the number of training sessions to four or five per week.

Anaerobic Training Zone

I have learned that anaerobic training can compliment aerobic and fat burning for individuals at advanced levels of training. This type of training is excellent for increasing muscle mass, definition, tone, increasing stamina, power, speed, endurance, and strength — all of which are important in developing a totally conditioned body. This type of exercise is extremely effective for developing the hips, thighs, hamstrings, and calves.

In order to reach your Anaerobic Training Zone, you elevate the intensity of exercise to reach 85 to 100 percent of your maximum heart rate.

This is not something I recommend for any beginner.

Anaerobic exercises can be added to your training program as you progress in your fitness level. I like to use wind sprints for anaerobic training. I started with five to ten minutes of warm-up jogging, followed by a series of four, 40-yard sprints. Then I move up to four, 50-yard sprints, followed by two, 70-yard sprints, I finished with one, 100-yard sprint then cool down with a slow jog for five to ten minutes.

My Favorite

Cardiovascular Exercise Options for General Conditioning

There are many different forms of cardiovascular/aerobic exercise. Yet all are not created equal. Some are better suited for specific training goals.

Treadmill walking tends to be a great choice for burning body fat. Jogging is best for building aerobic conditioning, and wind sprints are the best for anaerobic training. I recommend that you incorporate a variety of exercises into your training program.

Aerobic

Training Exercises

The following is a partial list of many aerobic training options that I feel bring the most success since they can easily fit into the busiest lifestyle.

Treadmills — I recommend the treadmill first because it is a weight-bearing exercise. It's also the most natural, which makes it the easiest to learn.

Recumbent and Stationary Bikes — These are good because they are easy to use, easy on the body, and excellent for getting your heart rate up. They are also relatively inexpensive and can fit nicely into the corner of the family room.

Step Climbers are more challenging. They don't work the upper body the way the treadmill does. They also require more athletic ability and coordination than a bike or treadmill.

Fat Burning Exercises

The treadmill is also my first recommendation for fat burning. It forces you to keep a steady pace and stride. When people walk outside they have a tendency to slow down; traffic, neighbors, and dogs often force you to break stride.

You can also jog at a slow pace on the treadmill, on the street, or on the track.

Good fat burning exercises include:
- ♦ Walking on the treadmill
- ♦ Jogging (slow pace) on the treadmill, street, or track
- ♦ Stationary biking — either upright or recumbent

Anaerobic Training

This type of exercise is high intensity, and requires all out effort. You shouldn't rush to add this type of training into your routine until you have had several good months, and in some cases years, under your belt.

Anaerobic exercises are:

♦ Sprinting on the treadmill
♦ Wind Sprints at the track
♦ Hill climbing — out in nature or on the treadmill
♦ Stationary bike sprints
♦ Stadium bleacher running
♦ Interval running 220, 440

This is only a partial list of cardiovascular training exercises. These seem to be the ones that give the best results and that are most popular with my clients. Feel free to integrate any other cardiovascular exercises not mentioned here that allow you to reach your training goals into your program as well.

The Primary Focus
Remember, the number one goal for your aerobic training routine is to get your cardiovascular system in shape. Fat burning and anaerobic workouts can be implemented later as you get into better shape. You'll still be burning many calories and losing some body fat.

Strive to train aerobically two or three times a week for at least 20 minutes. You can increase the length of your workout and the number of workouts as your fitness level increases. Remember, to listen to your body. If you get tired, dizzy, or faint, slow down or stop all together.

Aerobic/Weight Training Combinations
Optimally, you'll also be weight training as well. (We'll discuss weight training in the next chapter.) Here are my favorite combinations:

♦ Two training sessions, combining aerobics with weights
♦ Three training sessions — two aerobic/weight training sessions, and one solo aerobic session
♦ Three training sessions combining aerobic and weight training

The Recreational Activity Myth
Too often people believe that the recreational activities such as golf, strolling around the neighborhood, beach volleyball, noncompetitive swimming, and shooting basketball produce cardiovascular benefits. These activities

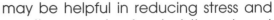

may be helpful in reducing stress and they may be fun, but they do not work the heart and lungs hard enough to produce aerobic, fat burning, or anaerobic benefits.

Recreational activities should be reserved for those "times off," when you give your mind and body a rest from the stresses of the day, as well as your usual training program.

An Important Ingredient
Cardiovascular exercise is very important for general fitness training and sports performance. It conditions and strengthens your heart and lungs; helps build endurance and stamina; and it is the best way to control weight and body fat. Cardiovascular exercises also promote muscular growth and aids recovery.

The Secrets of Aerobics
- Understand the different training zones and effectively apply them to your training goals.
- Get enough cardiovascular training to keep your heart and lungs in shape.
- Use the cardiovascular training split method consisting of warmup, weights, cool down.
- Find exercises that you enjoy, and that are relatively comfortable to perform.
- Change your exercises frequently.
- Vary the intensity, time, and length of your training sessions.
- Remember: A steady diet of the same exercise will eventually lead to mental and physical burnout.

The **5** Basics of Weight Training

It's important to know how and why weight training works before you pick up a weight. When muscles are subjected to resistance, they become more efficient, stronger, better toned. They develop increased blood flow and are less likely to ache or become injured. Exercising muscles properly counteracts muscular atrophy which occurs as we age. (The average man loses 50 percent of his muscle mass between 18 and 65 years of age.) Weight training exercises place a demand on the muscles, and as the muscles adapt to that demand, they become stronger and better able to sustain muscular activity.

Scientists are unable to tell us everything about resistance training; however, they do know that skeletal muscles are made up of thousands of muscle fibers and each fiber consists of many muscles strung end to end. When a muscle is subjected to resistance, it tears itself down and then rebuilds itself stronger than before to handle the resistance. That means when you subject your muscles to enough resistance to cause muscle fatigue, the muscles will be forced to rebuild themselves becoming stronger, more toned, and better able to handle more stress.

Your muscular system plays a major role in enabling you to perform the basic tasks of daily living; therefore, you must keep this system in proper working order so that you can keep on going comfortably and efficiently, whether you're striving for a gold medal or merely trying to stay on top of your studies and your social life. You keep your muscular system in top working order by adopting a good weight training program.

Three Forms of Resistance Training

Weight training falls under the umbrella of resistance training — isometric, isotonic, and isokinetic.

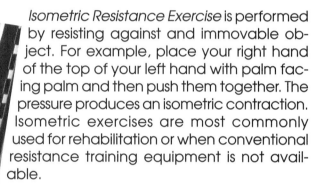

Isometric Resistance Exercise is performed by resisting against and immovable object. For example, place your right hand of the top of your left hand with palm facing palm and then push them together. The pressure produces an isometric contraction. Isometric exercises are most commonly used for rehabilitation or when conventional resistance training equipment is not available.

In *Isotonic Resistance Exercise* there is resistance against equal tension, such as when lifting free weights or barbells. When you perform an isotonic exercise, such as a barbell arm curl, as you raise the barbell from the starting position to the ending position, the resistance throughout the plane of travel does not stay the same. Though the actual weight of the barbell doesn't change, the lift becomes either easier or harder as it progresses because of the body's natural mechanical advantage, called "leverage." In isotonic lifting movements there is no accommodating resistance.

Isokinetic Resistance Exercises are most

commonly performed on weight machines, such as those manufactured by Paramount and Cybex. With these types of machines, the accomodation resistance is varied by the use of cam, cables, pulleys, or the slide lever principle. These machines are designed to meet the body's natural strength curves by changing the amount of resistance throughout the movement. The end result is that the tension feels equal throughout the entire range of motion.

All three forms of resistant training are important in developing a completely balanced physique. I'll be recommending exercises from each of these three areas, but I'll be dropping the fancy technical terms for all but isometrics. Isotonic will be referred to as training with free weights; isokinetic as training with weight machines.

Weight Training Concepts

There are many different ways you could train with weights. For instance a powerlifter trains to get stronger to be able to lift the heaviest weight possible. A football player lifts weights to become bigger, stronger, and a faster, better athlete. The way a bodybuilder trains with weights, however, comes closest to the type of training you'll be undertaking by following the principles in this book. What I feel works best combines the focus of power lifting, sports training, and bodybuilding.

A bodybuilder lifts weights to build muscle mass, shape, tone, and enhance muscular development what I refer to as perfect body weight training or training for self-development. The goal is to use weights to train the body for shape, definition, muscle mass, symmetry, proportion, strength, and power.

But before we actually get started with a program, it will be helpful to become familiar with the following definitions which I use frequently throughout this book.

Workout: a session of training. It can also be called a routine, program, or training schedule. A workout refers to the mental or written list of what you actually plan to do during your training session.

An *Exercise* is each individual movement performed in your routine.

Repetition or rep refers to one complete lifting movement. You perform one rep of an arm curl for example, by holding one free weight in each hand, arms down by your sides; then contract your arm muscles and raise the weights forward toward your shoulders. When the weights reach shoulder level, lower them back to the starting position at your sides. Reps are the number of completed lifting movements from start to finish.

Set is the number of reps completed in succession. For example if you perform ten complete reps of arm curls, rest for a moment, then performed ten more reps of arm curls, you will have completed two full sets.

Rest interval is the recovery time between reps and sets. It usually varies anywhere from thirty seconds to five minutes depending on your condition and goals.

Weight refers to the actual pounds lifted or pressed.

Lifting motion has been defined as the plane of travel or the arc of movement. There are two planes of travel: the concentric or positive portion of movement and the eccentric or negative portion. The muscles shortens as it develops tension to overcome the resistance in the positive portion of a movement. During the negative portion, the muscle lengthens while developing tension. For instance in the arm curl exercise, the downward part of the lift is the negative.

* You'll want to be in control of the weight both in the positive and negative portions of the movements. This will allow you to achieve the full benefit from the exercise.

Feel is the sensation you get in your muscles as you perform an exercise. Tightness, firmness, swelling, and burning are all good reactions to resistance training.

The most important feeling is the pump, which is that swollen feeling you get in your muscles toward the end of a set. Muscle pump is caused by the rapid movement of blood into the muscles to remove fatigue toxins, while replacing supplies of fuel and oxygen. When you succeed at creating a good muscle pump, you have worked a muscle or muscle group optimally.

Burn is caused by a rapid build-up of fatigue toxins in a muscle, and it is a good indication that you have worked a muscle or muscle group optimally. Extending repetitions past the pump stage will produce a burn.

Three Important Goals of Weight Training

It would be pointless to go into a gym and just lift weights without any rhyme or reason. Yet that's just what most people do. However, for complete physical development, you should consider the three important goals of weight training.

1. Increase Strength, Power, and Build Muscle Mass

Muscle mass is the size of each muscle or muscle group. The purpose of muscle is to generate force which requires strength, and strength is the foundation of a perfect body. The best way to develop strength is by lifting relatively heavy weights for a low number of reps.

Low Number of Reps + Heavy Weights = Strength

2. Tone Muscle

By toning, you will define, shape, and cause your muscles to become symmetrical. Muscle definition is the degree to which the muscle is developed. Often it is referred to as muscularity.

Shape refers to the pleasing pattern in the lines of a muscle. Proportion refers to the overall relationship between the size and the degree of development of all body parts. Symmetry is balance between the right and left sides of the body.

Medium Number of Reps + Medium Weights = Muscle Tone

3. Muscular Endurance

The ability of a muscle to produce force repeatedly over an extended period is considered muscular endurance. Movements that require maximum force, such as weight training, quickly deplete energy stores, and if you are not accustomed to these movements, you will quickly grow weak, feeling like you ran into a wall. Developing muscular endurance is very important because it enables you to complete more reps.

High Number of Reps + Light Weights = Muscular Endurance

Proper attention to developing strength, toning muscles, and increasing muscular endurance will encourage complete body development, give you the healthiest results, and get you into the best shape.

General Conditioning Weight Training Program

For weight training to be effective, you must perform the exercises properly. The best way to learn proper execution is by starting with the basics.

You should think of your initial attempts at weight training as a discovery phase. It's a time when you'll discover a great many things about yourself, as well as exercises work for you and those that don't.

It's important to remember when weight training that more is not always better. Our goal in weight training is not to build huge muscles so that you can kick sand in somebody's face.

The goals of the Sound Weight Training Program should include:
- Build a solid foundation of strength, muscle mass, power, muscle tone, symmetry, and endurance.
- Learn the basics of weight training exercise, techniques, and routines.
- Rehabilitate injured, lagging, or weak muscles.

My Favorite

Weight Training Exercises for General Conditioning

There are literally thousands of weight training exercises. However, I have nine weight training exercises that I use for beginners which bring a great deal of success.

These are exercises performed on single station or selectorized weight machines — those found in most well-equipped health clubs or fitness centers. They are designed to perform primarily one exercise and operate using its own weight stack. These machines allow you to target a specific muscle or muscle group.

During the basic stages of weight training, it's not necessary that you study all the muscle groups in the body. As you progress into the intermediate and advanced stages, you may want to increase your knowledge. However for now, we'll concentrate on seven areas of the body: neck, chest, back, shoulders, arms, midsection, and legs

There are two classifications of weight training exercises —basic and isolation.

Basic exercises stress the largest muscle groups of the body — thighs, back, and chest — often in combination with smaller muscles. In basic weight training, you use moderate to heavy weights to build muscle mass, strength, and power. My favorite movements include the bench press, lat pulldowns, shoulder presses, and leg presses.

Isolation exercises stress a single muscle group or part of a single muscle. These exercises are good for shaping and defining muscle groups. Leg extensions and leg curls are examples of two fine exercises for shaping and defining the thighs.

Beginning Exercises

The following basic exercises are ones which you will most likely find beneficial to include in your training program.

Chest Press

The basic exercise for the chest is the bench press, sometimes called the chest press. This is sometimes called the king of the upper body exercise because it is one of the best exercises for the upper body. It primarily stresses the chest muscles with a secondary emphasis on the front of the shoulders and the back of the arms. You can perform this exercise on the chest press machine (shown below), or by using barbells, dumbbells, or a Smith machine.

Lat Machine Pulldown

The most basic exercise for the back is the lat machine pulldown. This exercise places direct stress on the upper muscle of the back and is famous for helping to develop the V-shape look of the body. The lat pulldown also helps tone and shape the biceps and forearm muscles.

Shoulder Press

The granddaddy of the shoulder exercises, the shoulder press involves pressing a weight overhead, stressing the entire shoulder girdle and putting secondary stress on the triceps.

Arm Curl

The arm curl is the most basic exercise for the biceps. It involves curling a barbell or dumbbell in a semicircular arc to a position just beneath the chin, then lowering it to the starting point in front of the hips.

Tricep Extension

This is the most basic exercise for the triceps, although tricep press movements are also good.

Leg Press

While the squat is by far the best exercise for the legs, it takes a great deal of control and balance that can only be acquired with experience. Therefore, I start beginners out with leg training on the leg press.

The leg press is performed on a machine. Very much like the squat, the leg press stresses the entire leg region without putting much pressure on the lower back. You do not have to balance the weight; therefore, it is safer to perform and allows you to build good foundation strength which will enable you to perform squats as you advance in your program.

Leg Extension

The leg extension is an isolation exercise that puts a strong emphasis on the upper thigh muscles — the quadriceps. Although it is not labeled as a basic exercise, I find it's helpful in the beginning stages of training.

 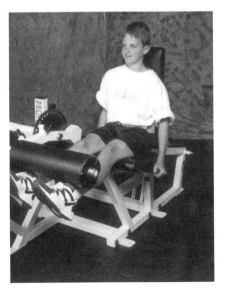

Leg Curl

The leg curl is also labeled an isolation exercise. It is the counterpart to the leg extension affecting the the upper rear or hamstring area.

 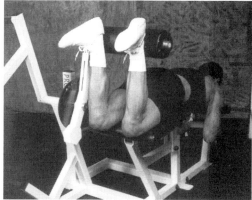

Standing Calf Raise

Calf exercises are often left out of many weight training programs, but they shouldn't be. In women, the underdevelopment of the calf can cause the thigh and hips to appear large, and pear shaped. Large deposits of fat in the calves can make the legs look short and dumpy.

For men, the calves are just as important, especially for defining the classic physique. Measurements of the neck, calves, and biceps are used to help determine the symmetry of the body. For sports, the calves are important in running, jogging, sprinting, and jumping.

4-Way Neck Isometrics

This is an isolation exercise that you can use to strengthen the neck muscles. It's an easy, safe way to strengthen the neck muscles and does not require any equipment.

Most people have underdeveloped or weak necks. This can prevent you from doing shoulder presses, squats, and stomach crunches. Therefore, it's important to develop your neck muscles.

Partial Incline Sit-Up

I haven't met anyone yet who is not concerned with the midsection or waist.

The partial incline sit-up uses only the upper 65 percent range of the sit-up movement. When performed correctly, this exercise stresses the upper and lower abdominals with no pressure on the lower back.

Hyperextensions

Lower back training is always essential at any level. It is extremely important in the beginning stages of training because a weak lower back will eventually become a big problem. The Hyperextension is excellent for strengthening the lower back region. It is easy and safe, and requires no equipment, so it can be performed anywhere.

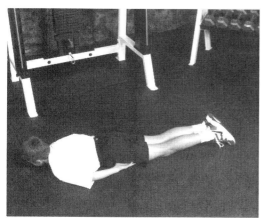 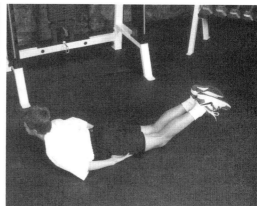

General Conditioning Goals

Beginners should train for muscle tone and muscular endurance. This is accomplished by performing ten to twenty-five repetitions of each exercise. It is not a good idea to train for muscle strength, power, and mass as a beginner. After you gain experience, develop balance, and good weight lifting form, you can begin experimenting with heavier weights.

First things first — keep your focus on familiarizing yourself with the exercise and pay attention on how your body is responding to the training.

Weight Training Techniques

Weight Training techniques are the specific ways in which you perform weight training movements. At the beginner level, I have five favorites.

Same Weight Straight Sets

This is a good technique to use while learning the groove or movement of each lift. To perform this technique, use a moderate amount of weight and perform the lifting exercise for three sets, with ten to fifteen reps per set. The weight remains the same for each set. After completing three sets, move onto the next exercise. This technique is excellent for teaching form because by lifting the same amount of weight throughout the three sets, you are able to concentrate more on technique than on how much weight you are lifting.

Example:
1 set 10-15 reps with 100 pounds
1 set 10-15 reps with 100 pounds
1 set 10-15 reps with 100 pounds

Isolation Sets
This technique works a muscle or muscle group completely before moving onto another muscle or muscle group.

Example:
Perform one set of eight reps on the leg press machine.
Rest thirty seconds.
Perform a second set.
Rest thirty seconds.
Perform a third set, and then move onto a new exercise.

Progressive Overload
This is really the goal behind weightraining. Making your muscles work harder is the basis behind building strength, toning muscles, and increasing muscular endurance. In performing this technique, you overload the muscles by steadily increasing the poundage, and/or by adding sets and reps throughout the sequence of lifts. You may also perform this technique by increasing the frequency of weight training sessions, changing exercises, or using a variety of techniques.

Circuit Training
This is very popular with beginners. When you perform a series of weight training exercises in a circuited manner — one after another — with little rest in between reps and sets, you are engaged in circuit training. Here you will go through a series of weight machines, working each body part for one set, then repeating the circuit for another set or sets. This training technique produces cardiovascular benefit and develops muscle endurance. It's popular because it saves time.

Priority (Weak Muscle) Training
Sometimes you must strengthen one muscle before you can train other muscles. For example, many people have weak neck muscles that won't allow them to do abdominal work. In order to work up to doing enough

stomach crunches to work the abs, these people must first strengthen their neck muscles by giving the weak or lagging muscle special attention.

For instance in the case of a weak neck, I suggest adding several sets of 4-way isometrics at the end of each training session. I also have a weak rear deltoid muscle (back side of my shoulder) which is not as developed as the rest of my shoulder muscles (front and middle deltoids); therefore, I train my lagging muscle first when my attention and energy level are high. Some people center their entire workout around developing an underdeveloped or weak muscle or muscle group.

My Favorite Training Routines

Your training routine is the complete program you do during a single training session, including all of the aerobic training and weight training exercises.

At the beginning stages, I recommend that you train two to three times per week with a day or two of rest between each workout. Your lifestyle and goals will be factors in determining the routine you select. Your routine should be comfortable and fit easily into your lifestyle. Setting up a routine which creates anxiety is a sure road to failure. You'll either skip workouts or quit training all together.

Of course with any new habit, it may take some time to get used a new routine. So give your training a chance before throwing in the towel.

I usually recommend the two day a week routine or the three-day a week routine.

The two-day routine can be:
   Monday-Thursday
   Tuesday-Friday
   Wednesday-Saturday

The two-day routine works well for those who have little time to devote to training, have limited access to training facilities, or who aren't overly concerned about weight loss. This is an especially good routine for beginners. Here, the entire body is trained at each workout.

The three-day routine can be:

Monday, Wednesday, Friday
Tuesday, Thursday, Saturday
Wednesday, Friday, Sunday

Three-day routines works better for people who want to lose body fat, get in shape quicker, and enjoy training. Generally, you'll train a different part of the body each day. For instance:

Workout 1 - chest, shoulders, legs, abs
Workout 2 - light legs, calves, abs, biceps, triceps
Workout 3 - back, legs, abs, calves.

Sets, Reps, Weight, Intensity

Throughout the beginning program, you'll be required to do one weight training exercise per body part during each training session. For the first few sessions, do only one set per exercise. Then, as you gain confidence and become more comfortable with the exercises, you'll want to increase the number of sets until you reach four sets per exercise.

Keep your repetitions in the 10 to 15 rep range for the chest, shoulders, back, biceps, triceps, and thighs. Twelve to 25 reps work best for the neck, abdomen, lower back, and calves.

Keep the intensity of your workouts moderate by choosing weights that allow you to perform in the desired repetition range.

Breathing and Rest Between Sets

Much has been written about the way you should breath when performing a weight lifting movement. I simply recommend that you breath naturally. However, it may be helpful to exhale during the upward part of the movement or the positive portion of the lift. During the downward or negative portion of the lift, you should inhale.

Just don't hold your breath. Holding your breath cuts off oxygen to the brain and could cause you to pass out. (Not a good idea when you're holding weights in each hand.)

A way to synchronize your breathing pattern is to breath in as you lower the weigh, then say "ooh" or "ahh" as you raise the weight. Making that funny little sound will force you to exhale and prevent you from holding your breath.

Resting between reps is very important. Specific training techniques requires different rest periods between reps. For instance, training for strength, power, and mass requires all-out effort, which in turn, increase the need for rest, usually two to four minutes of rest between sets. Training for muscle tone, using a moderate amount of weight, will require between one to two minutes of rest. Training for muscular endurance will require a rest period of only thirty seconds to one minute.

Your current condition will also dictate how much rest you need between sets. As you get into better shape, the need for rest will decrease. A good rule to follow is when you start to recover your breath, begin the next set. It will help you work at your current level of conditioning. As you get into better shape, the rest period adjusts naturally because the better condition you're in, the faster you recover.

A Final Note

General conditioning weight training is a time to learn how to lift weights. It's not a time to see how much weight the bar can hold. Rather, you should focus on learning the exercises, executing the movements, and getting a handle on your strengths and weaknesses. It's also a time for you to learn about your body and how it responds to weight training.

7
Nutrition for the Teenager

The teen years are a period of rapid growth for both boys and girls. And because this is often a period of high activity as well, eating a balanced, nutritional diet is absolutely essential.

By developing good nutritional habits early in life, you will reap many benefits later on. These habits will also allow you to grow and develop optimally; have increased physical energy and mental clarity; and also improve your physical appearance.

Ultimately, you are responsible for everything that goes into your mouth. You can't push the responsibility onto your parents, coaches, or the school lunchroom cooks. This means you need to:

- ◆ Learn the basic principles of nutrition
- ◆ Get an understanding of how foods affect your body
- ◆ Learn how to eat correctly and effectively

Basics of Nutrition

It is estimated that there are approximately fifty nutrients in food that are believed to be essential for the body's growth, maintenance, and repair. These are found in carbohydrates, fats, and proteins, which provide the body with energy. They are also found in vitamins, minerals, and water which are essential for your body to function in peak performance. If your body is deficient in even one of these components, you can become fatigued, become ill, even gain weight.

Carbohydrates

Simple and complex carbohydrates are a primary source of fuel for your body. Your body does not require a lot of simple carbohydrates, such as honey, sucrose, and table sugar. Simple carbohydrates cause a dramatic rise in blood sugar level creating an overproduction of insulin. Not good. Too much insulin takes too much sugar out of the bloodstream and causes you to feel tired and weak. It may also create an increase in fat deposition. On the other hand, complex carbohydrates, such as grains, pasta, potatoes and other vegetables, are broken down more slowly in the digestive system causing a more gradual increase in blood sugar level. The result is that you have more productive energy for a longer period.

To fuel your body properly, you should eat mostly complex carbohydrates and avoid the simple carbohydrates — sugars, cakes, and candies.

Proteins

Proteins are essential for the growth and maintenance of all body tissue. They serve as a major source of building material for muscle, blood, skin, hair and nails, and for the internal organs, primarily the heart and brain. They also produce hormones that regulate a host of bodily functions, including growth, metabolic rates, sexual development, and antibodies that combat foreign substances in the body. During digestion, protein is broken down into simpler units called amino acids. In this state, amino acids enter a pool where they are stored for the body to draw upon when it needs new protein.

You get "good" protein from eggs, milk, chicken, and turkey, and "bad" protein from fatty, red meats. With the exception of water, your body contains more protein than any other substance.

Complete and Incomplete Proteins

Just as all carbohydrates are not created equal, neither are protein foods. Therefore, you need to pay particular attention to the protein sources. There are incomplete and complete sources of protein. Incomplete protein sources are those foods that don't provide a good essential amino acid balance, such as fruits and vegetables. Complete protein sources are most meats and dairy products.

Fats

Fats are a secondary source of energy. Contrary to popular opinion, you should not eliminate fats completely from your diet because some fats are good for you. After your body has depleted all of the available stored muscle glycogen, it calls on fats to supply needed energy. Furthermore, fats carry and absorb the fat soluble vitamins A, D, E, and K. Fats supply the body with energy during periods of inactivity or rest and during aerobic exercises. It surrounds and protects vital organs — the kidneys, heart and liver. And finally, fat provides a blanket for preserving heat in the body.

Sodium

Sodium is necessary because it helps in transmitting nerve impulses. Too little sodium in your diet could cause severe cramping and weakness. But don't run over and pick up the salt shaker! It's easy to overdose on sodium in this country. The typical American diet contains more than ten times the minimum requirement of salt. That means it is highly unlikely that you are now, or will in the near future, become sodium deficient.

Most experts recommend 2,500-3,000 milligrams of sodium per day. A lunch of chips or fries, cheeseburger with condiments, commercial size pickle and flavored milk shake contains approximately 3,500 milligrams of sodium. That means that most people use up their allotted daily sodium intake in one meal!

If you eat good food, in its most natural state, you will get an adequate supply of sodium without ever having to reach for a salt shaker. And you will avoid the effects of excess sodium in your diet such as bloating, which can lead to lethargy.

Vitamins

Vitamins are organic food substances that the body cannot manufacture. They contribute to the biochemical reactions that convert food into energy and assist in forming bone and tissue. Each vitamin has a specific task. It isn't necessary to define each one at this time; however, the important thing to remember is that if you're deficient in all or part of a single vitamin, your body's biochemical reactions may be changed causing you some major problems.

The best sources for vitamins are: fresh green and yellow vegetables, fresh fruits, whole grains, fish, poultry, and meat. To ensure that you're getting all of the vitamins you need, I strongly suggest that you consider taking a daily multivitamin.

Minerals

Found in a wide range of plant and animal foods and in fresh drinking water, minerals are organic elements in their simplest form. As with vitamins, if you lack just one mineral, your body will not function properly. Minerals combine with vitamins to form enzymes that are necessary to nearly every physiological process, as well as all body tissues and internal fluids. In short, you need minerals for your body to function at peak performance. That's why you hear, "Take your vitamins and minerals every day." Minerals are not secondary supplements. They are essential elements for maintaining a healthy, active body.

Water

Water makes up nearly 60 percent of your total body weight and is essential for:

+ proper digestion,
+ proper absorption,
+ proper circulation,
+ proper elimination,
+ transportation of nutrients,
+ maintenance of body temperature,
+ maintenance of the electrolyte balance your body needs for survival, and
+ the healthy functioning of every living cell.

Vigorous physical activity causes heavy sweating — the loss of body fluid/water. Evaporation of sweat on the skin is the body's natural, built-in cooling system. However, with this loss of water comes a loss of electrolytes — ionized salts in the blood, tissue fluids and cells, including sodium, potassium, and chlorine. The depletion of these elements can cause metabolic and/or neurological difficulties.

Therefore, it is vitally important that you drink plenty of water! Most experts recommend six to eight glasses per day. During hard training, I suggest that you drink plenty of water. Have a glass next to you all day long, and sip it often.

No nutrient acts alone. They must all be present for your body to function well at peak performance. How much is enough for you? That depends on your age, sex, size, and activity level. Good nutrition means providing your body with proper nutrients in proper amounts so that you can go about the task of daily performance.

Balancing It Out

The body works best when you feed it the right combination of food. The question is how do you do that? The answer is by eating a variety of food from each of the four major food groups: meats, fish, and poultry; fruits and vegetables; grains, nuts and cereal; and dairy products — and by determining what percentage of your total caloric intake must come from proteins, carbohydrates, and fat sources. It is impossible for anyone to give you an exact ratio of carbohydrates, proteins, and fats because we are all created just a little bit differently. It is up to you to experiment and discover these ratios for yourself.

To find your nutritional requirements, I recommend that you keep a food journal in which you can record your daily intake of food. In your journal you might include how you feel after eating each food. Do you feel energized or do you feel like you need a nap? Do you feel bloated or lean? This information will help you discover what food your body really needs.

Calories

A calorie is a measurement of the amount of energy contained in food. Proteins and carbohydrates contain approximately four calories per gram;

fats contain nine calories per gram. Though fats are the most efficient fuel when it comes to caloric density, they are the most undesirable if you are on a low-calorie program for weight control or weight reduction. If you take in more calories than your body can burn off, the excess is stored in the form of fat (adipose cells) distributed throughout the body.

It doesn't matter whether the excess is in the form of proteins, carbohydrates, or fats, your body will break it down and store it for a future time when it requires more energy than your food intake at that time is providing. Then, your body will retrieve and metabolize the fat in the adipose cells to make up the difference. If your body has all of the nutrients it needs to function optimally and if you are eating at least the minimum quantity of the various foods required at any given time by your digestive and energy producing systems, fat gain and fat loss are a matter of simple arithmetic. Unfortunately, most diets do not take these factors into consideration and that can cause a number of undesirable things to happen:

♦ Your body can begin to metabolize muscle tissue.
♦ Your body's ability to metabolize fat may be impaired.
♦ You may realize various vitamin and mineral deficiencies.
♦ You may experience a lack of energy.
♦ You may even develop some psychological problems.

Because of the possibility of these problems, any diet regime (whether for weight gain or loss) has to take into account the body's need for certain nutritional minimums and for a relative balance of various foods in the daily food intake. The diet must be balanced in order to cause a positive reaction. Balance is the key.

So, how important are calories? Food energy comes from carbohydrates, proteins and fats. Calories are a way of measuring the energy these nutrients provide. And there are two main points to consider in reference to calories:

♦ The maintenance of an ideal body weight
♦ Supplying an adequate amount of energy

Defining calories is really quite simple. The food you eat is converted into glycogen, and then stored in the muscles for fuel to be burned when you need it. Any excess calories are stored in the body as fat. The main question about calories is, "How many calories should I consume?" Again, that depends on individual factors such as: age, gender, height, weight, activity level, and individual metabolism. These varying conditions are precisely why it is impossible for one diet plan to work for everybody. These factors are different for each of us and that is why I stress the importance of individualism when developing a nutrition program.

Since most of the people I consult are concerned with losing body fat, I have seen a host of unhealthy "starvation methods." And it concerns me. Starving only creates more problems. It causes your body to feed on its own muscle causing you to lose muscle mass. Starvation also causes your metabolism to slow down making it even more difficult to burn fat. A good healthy nutrition program allows you to eat healthy foods in comfortable amounts for your body. In order to lose body fat, you need to feed your body steadily. Don't starve it. By feeding your body carefully and steadily, you will increase your metabolic rate, increase your body's ability to burn fat, and repair and build muscle.

To get a handle on how many calories your body burns, experiment with your calorie consumption and you will be on your way to mastering weight control. Even when you are inactive, your body still requires energy to repair and maintain cells, build muscle, and carry on basic functions, such as breathing and digestion. Therefore, it is crucial that you consume enough of the right kinds of calories to keep your body in top working order.

Calories are important to your training program in that too many calories can cause your body to retain fat; too few calories causes you to lose energy. And eating too much of a good thing can be bad as well. I have heard people say, "Eat all of the healthy food you want," or "I can have all of the fruit I want." Then, they set out to prove it by eating a whole

watermelon or a serving bowl of fruit. You can gain weight if you eat too much of any food. Overload your body with anything from lettuce to chocolate bars and your body will be forced to store the excess as fat. It's just that simple.

Eating and Training
Resistance training combined with cardiovascular training puts specific nutritional demands on the body. The amount of calories you burn when training depends on: your individual statistics (height, weight, etc.), the kind of activity you're doing, the intensity level of the activity, and the frequency of training sessions.

The important points to remember when selecting your foods are:

- Eat a variety of foods from each of the four major food groups: meats, fish, poultry; fruits and vegetables; grains and dairy products
- Eat the proper proportions of proteins, carbohydrates, and fats for your body.

Meals

When you eat is as important as what you eat. When setting up your eating program, give strong consideration to the following criteria: your training level, your lifestyle, and your goals. The keys to remember when structuring your eating plan is to spread your meals out over the course of the day and don't skip them.

Pretraining meals

The foods you consume before training will play a major part in how well you train. Pretraining meals help provide energy for your muscles and stock your system with fluids. They should consist of fruits, cooked vegetables, lean meats, and whole wheat breads. Pretraining meals are best eaten 1 1/2 to 2 hours before training. Pay careful attention to portions. Overeating causes loss of energy and bloating.

Pregame eating

The types of foods you eat before a game or an athletic event differ very little from the pretraining meals. In fact, if you are following a good, wholesome, nutritional eating plan, you needn't change your diet before training or a competition.

It's important to remember that what you eat each and every day affects your performance, not just the pretraining or pregame meals. If you don't eat a good diet consistently, your body will not be able to perform at optimal levels.

Getting Started

Your main nutritional concern should be to achieve a clean, balanced diet. This doesn't mean "going on a diet" in the old sense. Old-fashioned diets don't work. They rob your body of valuable nutrients, and they cause you to get fat.

Your body is a survival machine. Deprive it of nutrients and food, and it will find a way to survive. The body compensates for starvation by clinging to existing body fat, adding new body fat by slowing the metabolism, and inhibiting the body's natural body fat-burning process.

Nutrition doesn't have to be confusing. To become your own nutritionist, you need to get in touch with your body. You don't have to be a scientist to know that you shouldn't eat every bite on your plate even after your stomach feels full. You should be able to recognize signals, such as bloating, fullness, depression, lethargy, and anxiety. These are ways that your body uses to communicate with you about the negative effects of the foods you're eating. If you feel good, satisfied, and energetic after a meal, then you've found food that is good for your body.

In order to get in touch with your body's nutritional needs, you are going to have to get an overview of your existing nutritional habits. You begin by carefully analyzing several key points about your present diet.

The most critical components of nutrition center around:
- ♦ What you eat
- ♦ When you eat
- ♦ Why you eat
- ♦ Where you eat

The answers you come up with will expose your current nutritional patterns, which may not support your desire to reach peak performance.

Pay attention to what you eat. Read labels and record what you eat in your journal.

Why you are eating is probably the most important nutritional factor because it will tell you the real reason your body is in the shape it is now. Before you eat, ask yourself questions such as, "Am I really hungry?" Or "Am I just bored or lonely?" Or "Am I eating because my body needs fuel or energy?"

By tracking when you eat, you may be able to identify negative eating patterns, such as late night snacking. Do you eat most of your foods late in the day?

Where you eat refers to the actual location. Are you eating at fast food hamburger stands? School? Home?

These important journal entries will expose many of your nutritional problems — areas that need to be changed. But you won't have to change everything at once. This only causes unnecessary stress.

For starters just become aware of your nutritional habits. Eat at least three meals a day. And never skip breakfast.

Think of your body as a car. The foods you eat are the fuel. Carbohydrates and fats are like gasoline. Your body burns them for energy. Protein is like a building block and is responsible for building muscles. Vitamins and minerals derived from the foods you eat as well as supplements (which I discuss in Chapter 28) are like the wax on a car. They protect you from the elements. In cars this translates into rust and corrosion. For the body, this is illness and fatigue.

Figure Firming for Teenage Girls

Although both men, women, boys, and girls can train pretty much the same way — that is they can perform the same weight training and aerobic exercises and reap many of the same results — I found through my experience of training females that they can benefit with some special twists to their training program.

Adolescence is always a time of change, of asserting independence, and coping with peer pressure. For girls today, it just doesn't mean leaving childhood behind but often losing self-esteem in the face of images forced upon them by society.

The current "vogue" look of the models with their sunken cheeks and muscle toneless arms and legs is not only unattractive but unhealthy. A well-toned, shapely, energetic body is by in far much more attractive... and healthy.

I am somewhat concerned with teenage girls when it comes to diet and exercise. A recent survey conducted by *Shape* magazine surveyed girls ages 11-17 on their body image, exercise, and eating habits. The results were scary: many of the survey participants had serious eating disorders and constantly compared themselves to classmates with so-called "perfect bodies" — the ones researchers feared had the more serious eating disorders.

Excessive weight gain and loss of control of body shape can play havoc to your self-image. We all should strive to put our best foot forward, and that includes our physical appearances. An exercise program consisting of weight training, aerobic conditioning, and good nutritional practices is the best way to improve your appearance.

Way to Shape the Female Body

Generally teenage girls are worried most about controlling body fat, so "diet" is often first the course of action. And what usually follows is a host of problems from eating disorders, to damaging weight loss, depression, and loss of energy and drive. Then follows a rebound of body fat gain. This scenario becomes a never-ending cycle as every new year brings a new miracle "weight loss" program, product, or pill.

The answer
The muscles in the body give it its shape and contour. The best way to add shape, symmetry, and tone is through a good training program.

"Figure Firming" Program
Figure Firming guides you though a routine designed to concentrate on the areas of "concern," including hips, thighs, upper arms, and abs. The end result will be a firmer, more proportionate shapely figure. The goals are to lose body fat, develop symmetry and proportion, increase muscle tone, and enhance shape.

"Figure Firming" Routine
Monday — chest, triceps, abs, aerobic training
Tuesday — legs, abs, fat burning
Wednesday — back, biceps, abs, aerobic training
Thursday — shoulders, abs, fat burning
Friday — legs, abs, aerobic training

Monday

Smith Machine Chest Press

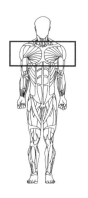

Incline Dumbbell Flys

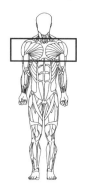

Tricep Cable Pushdown

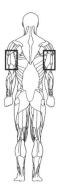

Shaping For Girls

S
h
a
p
i
n
g

For

G
i
r
l
s

Bench Dip

Crunch

Incline Seated Leg Raise

Tuesday

Smith Machine Squat

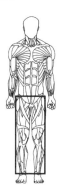

One-leg Leg Press

Smith Machine Standing Calf Raise

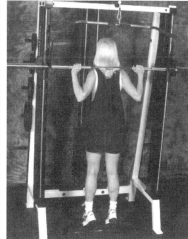

Shaping for Girls

S h a p i n g For **G i r l s**

Calf Raise on Leg Press Machine

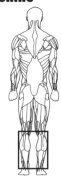

Partial Incline Sit-up

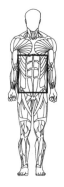

Hanging Leg Raise

Lat Pulldown

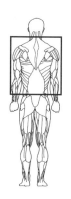

Tuesday

Low Pulley Cable Row

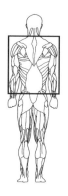

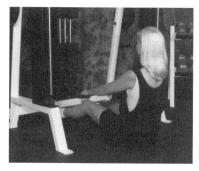

Dumbbell Arm Curl

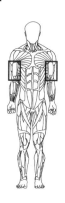

Shaping For **Girls**

Crunch

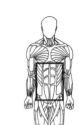

 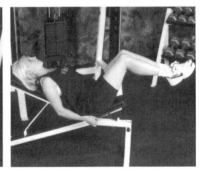

Incline Seated Leg Raise

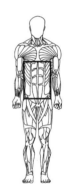

Smith Machine Shoulder Press (front of neck)

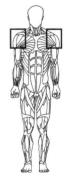

Dumbbell Lateral Raise

Dumbbell Front Raise

Partial Incline Sit-up

Shaping for Girls

Shaping
For
Girls

Hanging Leg Raise

Leg Press

Dumbbell Squat

Leg Extension

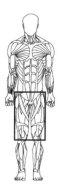

Leg Curl

Smith Machine Standing Calf Raise

Shaping for Girls

89

S
h
a
p
i
For
G
n
i
r
g
l
s

Calf Raise on Leg Press

Crunch

Incline Seated Leg Raise

"Figure Firming" Poundages & Weight

All Upper Body Exercises
Increase weight 5-10 lbs. per set

Lower body exercises — Leg Press, Squat, Calf Raise
Increase weight 10-20 lbs. per set

Leg Extension and Leg Curl
Increase weight 5-10 lbs. per set

Nonweight Assisted Exercises — Abdominals, Hyperextensions
Exercise to failure

"Figure Firming" Sets & Reps

Upper Body Exercises
Between 12-15 reps per set

Lower Body Exercises
Between 15-25 reps per set

Number of sets per exercise

2-3

"Figure Firming" Rest Between Sets

 1-2 minutes

"Figure Firming" Techniques

Pyramid — increase the weight for each set while at the same time decreasing the number of reps you perform.

"Figure Firming"Aerobic Training

Monday after weights
Jog, treadmill, stationary bike, or row, etc. 20 minutes with heart rate in the 75% range

Tuesday after weights
Jog, treadmill, stationary bike, or row, etc. 35 minutes with heart rate in the 65% range

Wednesday after weights
Jog, treadmill, stationary bike or row, etc. 45 minutes with heart rate in the 55% range

Thursday after weights
Jog, treadmill, stationary bike or row, etc. 15 minutes with heart rate in the 75% range

Friday after weights
Jog, treadmill, stationary bike or row, etc. 30 minutes with heart rate in the 60% range

"Figure Firming" Stretching
Full body stretch after all weight training and aerobic workouts. (See Chapter 26 for key body stretches.)

9 Training for Weight Loss

As a teenager you may be faced with the same challenge that many adults face — too much body fat. I have been on this side of the coin more than once. I have probably lost close to over 200 pounds in my lifetime. For years I played the yo-yo game of gain weight, lose weight. When I was a junior in high school, I weighed 235 pounds. Over the course of that year, I went on a diet and exercise program, and I dropped my weight down to 205 pounds by the start of my senior year. So you can bet that I know just how you feel. I truly understand your desires to improve yourself. After I lost the weight, it made a drastic difference in my self-esteem. I felt better about myself, increased my energy triple fold, and was a much better athlete.

We all know that being overweight can be a hazard to our overall health. For athletes it can hinder performance and cause injuries. Today, the concern for teenagers is escalating. It seems every year more and more teenagers are reported as being overweight and out-of-shape. And the major cause — high fat, junk food diets combined with in-activity.

The teen years are a great time for a person to start learing how to take care of his or her body. After all evidence shows us that it doesn't get any easier when we get older. Start young and learn how to control your weight; it will make it much easier as your body ages and your lives become more complicated.

Warning — Weight Loss Can Be Hazardous to Your Health
Going on a diet, cutting back calories, losing weight, and changing the shape of the body is serious business. I have seen people who attempted this (in unhealthy ways) wind up in the hospital, suffer from eating disorders, cause permanent damage to their bodies, become depressed, even die from misguided, unhealthy practices of losing weight.

There is only one way to safely and effectively lose weight — stick to a good nutrition, exercise, and training program.

Forget what the ads say, forget about the magic potions, products, and pills.

My Favorite
Weight Loss and Body Shaping Training Program

It's pretty hard to tell someone who wants to lose a lot of weight to exercise three times per week, eat a sensible diet, and wait for the results to appear. When I was attempting to lose fifty pounds, I knew that that approach was not going to work for me. So I experimented and I discovered a workout that gave me fantastic results. By following it I was able to trim fifty pounds of body fat while at the same time toning, strengthening, and shaping my body.

I trained five days in a row, dividing the body up over five sessions. Each session consisted of weight training (training one major body part), abdominal training, and some form of aerobic conditioning. I followed this schedule Monday through Friday taking the weekends off for rest. However, I did not veg out and sit on the couch all weekend. I would usually do some form of recreational activity like riding my bike or playing basketball.

"Weight Loss" Training Routine

Monday — chest, abs, aerobic training
Tuesday — shoulders, abs, fat burning training
Wednesday — back, abs, aerobic training
Thursday — arms, abs, fat burning
Friday — legs, abs, aerobic training

Training For Weight Loss

Smith Machine Chest Press

Incline Dumbbell Press

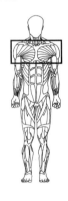

Dumbbell Flat Bench Flys

Smith Machine Decline Press

Crunch

Leg Raise

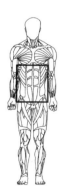

Training for Weight Loss

Training for Weight Loss

Smith Machine Shoulder Press

Dumbbell Shoulder Press

Smith Machine Upright Row

Dumbbell Front Raise

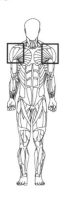

Cable Crunch

Hanging Leg Raise

Training For Weight Loss

T
r
a
i
n
i
n
g

For

W
e
i
g
h
t

L
o
s
s

Broomstick
Twists

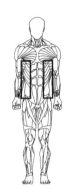

Wednesday

Lat Machine
Pulldown

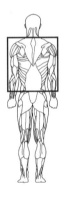

Seated Low
Pulley Row

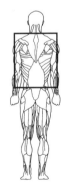

Reverse Smith Upright Row

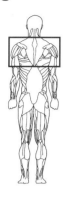

Hyperextension

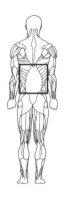

Incline Partial Sit-up

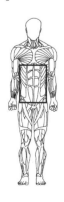

Training For Weight Loss

Training For Weight Loss

Reverse Crunch

  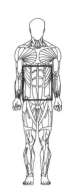

Thursday

Barbell Arm Curl

Low Pulley Arm Curl

Smith Machine Close Grip Press

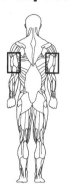

Bench Dips

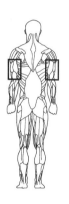

Crunches

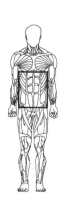

Training for Weight Loss

Training for Weight Loss

Incline Knee-ups

Friday

Leg Press

Smith Machine Squat

  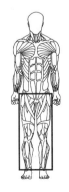

Leg Extension

Leg Curl

Smith Machine Standing Calf Raise

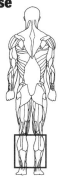

Training For Weight Loss

  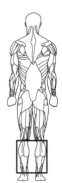

Calf Raise (on Leg Press)

  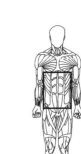

Crunch

  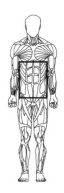

Leg Raise

Weight Loss Sets & Reps
1st exercise on each day
1st set 12 reps
2nd set 8 reps
3rd set 6 reps

2nd and consecutive exercises
1st set 10 reps
2nd set 8 reps

Weight Loss Poundages
All Upper Body Exercises
Increase weight 5-10 lbs. per set

Lower Body Exercises — Leg Press, Squat, Calf Raise
Increase weight 10-20 lbs. per set

Leg Extension and Leg Curl
Increase weight 5-10 lbs. per set

Nonweight assisted exercises — Abdominals and Hyperextensions
Exercise to failure

"Weight Loss" Rest Between Sets
1-2 minutes

"Weight Loss" Techniques
Pyramid — Increase the weight for each set while at the same time decreasing the number of reps you perform.

"Weight Loss" Aerobic Training
Monday after weights
Jog, treadmill, stationary bike, or row, etc. 20 minutes with heart rate in the 75% range

Tuesday after weights
Jog, treadmill, stationary bike, or row, etc. 35 minutes with heart rate in the 65% range

Wednesday after weights
Jog, treadmill, stationary bike or row, etc. 45 minutes with heart rate in the 55% range

Thursday after weights
Jog, treadmill, stationary bike or row, etc. 15 minutes with heart rate in the 75% range

Friday after weights
Jog, treadmill, stationary bike or row, etc. 30 minutes with heart rate in the 60% range

"Weight Loss" Stretching
Full body stretch after all weight training and aerobic workouts.
(See Chapter 26 for key body stretches.)

"Weight Loss" Special Training Notes
Remember the goal is to safely lose body fat. Include these guidelines in your program:

- Shoot to lose no more than 2 pounds a week, preferably 1 pound a week.
- Get body fat tested, find out lean body mass.
- Chart and monitor your weight loss weighing in twice a week.
- Include supplements in your diet (see Chapter 28).
- Get plenty of rest .
- Don't use rubber suits to "sweat it out".

Sometimes it happens — you overexercise and diet to excess. Here are the warning signs:

- Irritability
- Loss of appetite
- Dizziness/lightheadedness
- Loss of focus, concentration
- Continued loss of weight
- Weakness
- Soft muscles
- Losing more than 3-4 pounds a week

Nutrition and Weight Loss
What you put into your mouth is going to determine about 70 percent of your success while on a weight loss program. As the saying goes, "You can out eat any exercises program." Work in the gym is a given, but you will have to work equally as hard on your nutritional program in order to succeed. You will have to learn:

- The basics of nutrition (see Chapter 7)
- How foods affect your body
- How to prepare meals
- When to eat
- What to eat
- Where to eat
- Why you should eat.
- Supplements, vitamins, and minerals

Set Up a System of Checks and Balances

Most teenagers that are concerned with their weight don't need fancy body fat tests to tell them when they are overweight. Most see it in the mirror and feel the effects. I know this all too well myself. As a junior in high school, I weighed 235 pounds I didn't need a test to tell me. I saw my stomach sticking out in the mirror and felt bloated, fatigued, and unmotivated.

However, I think it is a good idea if possible to get tested to see what your body fat percentage is and to periodically get tested during your training and weight loss program.

Safe effective weight loss is a lot more than just lowering the numbers on the scale. There is a huge difference between losing body fat and losing muscle mass. One of the first things you need to learn about both weight loss and weight gain is the difference between:

- Lean muscle mass
- Body Fat

Good Ways to Safely Gauge Weight Loss

There are Informal methods: photographs, videotaping, tape measures, and scales. These are easy to use and require little time and effort. I feel they are probably the most practical for nearly everyone.

Scientific methods include muscular fitness tests, cardiovascular fitness tests, and body composition analysis. These offer a more scientific measurement of your progress and seem to appeal to people who are more statistically minded and like cold, hard facts.

Photographs are my favorite method of measuring my progress because they allow me to see my body as it really is. With photographs, you can get a 360 degree view of your body, providing a realistic perspective on how it looks from every angle. Photographs also give you a permanent record of what your body looked like at a specific time.

The easiest, quickest, least time-consuming and most economical way to gauge your progress is to simply look in the mirror. The mirror gives us the opportunity to "catch a glimpse" of our progress any time we wish.

However, there are some drawbacks with using the mirror as a gauging tool. It is only natural to focus on what we want to see. Some people focus on the good areas. Whereas, others will not see their progress because they can't get past looking at the areas that haven't changed shape. Another problem is that unless you are able to purchase a special three-way mirror or set up a series of mirrors, you will only be able to see a limited view of yourself.

I recommend using the mirror for day-to-day feedback. It's a pretty good judgment of your actual progress.

The tape measure is a popular method for gauging progress because it gives a reading of your body size. A scale can give you total pounds lost or gained, but the tape measure precisely provides the size of each area of your body.

The Key Points to Follow When Using a Tape Measure
- Use the same tape measure every time.
- Use a cloth tape measure -- plastic tape measures eventually stretch and won't give accurate measurements.
- Have the same person measure you each time.
- Record all measurements to the closest sixteenth of an inch. Take measurements before working out.
- Relax your muscles while they are being measured
- Take measurements in the middle of the muscle.
- Don't pull the tape too tight or let it hang too loose.
- Always measure the same area.

Twelve key measurements to take:

- Neck
- Biceps (right and left)
- Forearm (right and left)
- Chest

- ♦ Waist
- ♦ Hips
- ♦ Thighs (right and left)
- ♦ Calves (right and left)

I like to use measurements to determine if the body is losing weight evenly throughout. However, tape measurements can be very misleading if you only pay attention to inches lost or gained. Measurements can't show whether you're losing muscle mass or body fat. They can only denote that a change has occurred.

The scale is probably the most widely used piece of equipment for gauging progress. Unfortunately, it is the most misleading and inaccurate. Scales do not make a distinction between body fat and lean muscle mass. So if the scale shows you have lost ten pounds, have you lost ten pounds of muscle mass or body fat? Body fat weighs less than muscle mass. Therefore, when you weigh five pounds more yet measure inches smaller, have you gained or lost? My best advice is to throw away your scale!

Body Fat Tests

If you're like most people on any training program, you want to increase your lean body mass and decrease your body fat. It is possible to gauge your progress in this area by monitoring your body composition. Sophisticated tests can tell you how much lean body mass and how much body fat you have. All of the available methods used for this type of measurement require a different level of commitment, time, and expense, and offer varying degrees of accuracy. None of the tests are perfect, although some are better than others.

The best body composition analysis test is the hydrostatic or underwater weighing analysis. This method is considered to be 98 percent accurate. Hydrostatic body composition analysis must be performed by a special technician in a special "dunk tank," and usually costs $50 to $100.

The caliper test (skin fold) is the most popular method for gauging body composition. This method, used by colleges, sports teams, and health clubs should be performed by a knowledgeable technician. The results are found by taking about seven skin fold measurements from various parts of the body. The technician then manipulates these numbers according to a formula to determine your approximate body fat percentage. Though this method has proven effective over the years, it is only as accurate as the operator administering it. So check out the technician's credentials, and try to use the same person for your test each time.

These tests may seem rather elaborate for something most of us can do just by looking in the mirror and being honest with ourselves. However, athletes, bodybuilders, and fitness enthusiasts have used body composition analysis for years to ensure their success. Yet many others who have not taken advantage of these tests have reached the same success levels of those who have.

Whether you choose to use these tests as a gauge of your progress is strictly up to you.

Training for
Weight Gain

Although this may be hard for many people to believe, there are those that struggle with putting on weight just like those who struggle to take off weight. Today, it is hard for me to believe that after spending more than half my life training to lose weight and keep from gaining weight, that I now have to work very hard to keep my weight from dropping. I have gotten my system so efficient and tuned up, that I can easily lose weight. Because my body fat level is so low, when I lose weight now it is usually muscle mass — the weight that is not good to lose. So I have had to become very good at putting on quality weight (muscle mass) over the last five years.

Putting on weight can be important for those in sports or those who are naturally thin. when I talk about putting on weight, I am not referring to getting fat. I mean putting on quality weight — lean muscle mass — opposed to body fat.

Many people make the mistake of thinking that eating everything in sight is the way to gain weight or bulk up. Weight gain is only good if it is quality muscle mass.

The safest way to put on weight is gradually. At the most I like to shoot for about a pound or two every two weeks. This doesn't sound like much but a pound every two weeks is two pounds a month, which equals twenty-four pounds a year. That's a lot!

Even gaining one pound a month doesn't seem like much, but when you add it up it's a total of twelve pounds a year. Keep in mind that as a teen, you're growing rapidly, so a ten or even twenty pound weight gain over the course of a year may be realistic.

There are three important areas of consideration when training for weight gain: weight training, nutrition, and recovery.

My Favorite
Training Programs for Weight Gain

A consistent weight training program is essential to gaining quality, lean muscle mass. Weight training is the way you build muscle. And muscle is the quality weight that you want to gain. The best routines for gaining weight are those that involve basic movements, such as:
- Bench Press
- Seated Rows
- Power Clean
- Squats
- Leg Press

In other words, you're going to have to get after it in the weight room.

"Weight Gain" Training Routine

Monday — Heavy Upper Body
chest, back, shoulders, biceps,triceps, neck, abs
Tuesday — Heavy Lower Body
quadriceps, hamstrings, calves, lower back, abs
Thursday — Light Upper Body
chest, back, shoulders, biceps,triceps, neck, abs
Friday — Light Lower Body
quadriceps, hamstrings, calves, lower back, abs

Monday/Thursday — Upper Body

**Smith Machine
Chest Press**

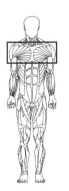

**Incline
Dumbbell Press**

**Lat Pulldown
Wide Grip
(behind the
neck)**

Training for Weight Gain

Training *For* **Weight Gain**

Low Pulley Cable Row

Smith Machine Shoulder Press (front of neck)

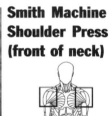

Smith Machine Upright Row

Smith Machine Shoulder Shrug

Barbell Arm Curl

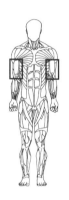  

Bench Dips

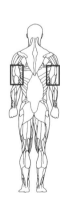  

Training for Weight Gain

Training for Weight Gain

4-Way Neck Isometrics

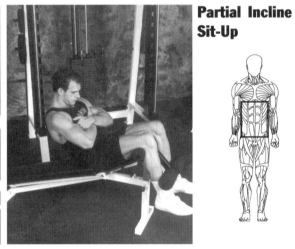

Partial Incline Sit-Up

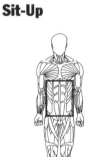

Hanging Leg Raise

Tuesday/Friday — Lower Body

Barbell Power Clean

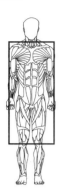

Leg Press

Smith Machine Squat

Training for Weight Gain

T r a i n
W e i g h t G a i n

 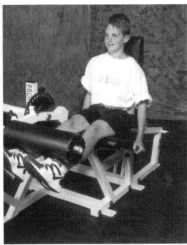

Leg Extension

Lying Leg Curl

Smith Machine Standing Calf Raise

Crunch

Incline Bench Knee-Ups

Hyperextension

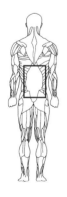

"Weight Gain" Sets & Reps
Monday/Tuesday — Heavy Day
3 sets of each exercise
1st set 10 reps, 2nd set 8 reps, 3rd set 6 reps

Thursday/Friday — Light Day
2 sets of each exercise
1st set 12 reps, 2nd set 8 reps

"Weight Gain" Poundages
All Upper Body Exercises
Increase weight 5-10 lbs. per set

Lower Body Exercises — Leg Press, Squat, Calf Raise
Increase weight 10-20 lbs. per set

Leg Extension and Leg Curl
Increase weight 5-10 lbs. per set

Nonweight Assisted Exercises — Neck Isos, Abdominals, Hyperextensions
Exercise to failure

"Weight Gain" Rest Between Sets
2 minutes

Exercise for Preteens

Almost daily, I am asked by concerned parents about what I feel is the right age for a young person to start training seriously, particularly with weights. Although I must admit I do not know the answer to this based on scientific data, research, and laboratory tests, I do have what I consider to be more valuable evidence — personal experience. Remember, I started a serious weight training ("supervised") program at age 14, when I was in the eighth grade.

In my day it was extremely controversial for teenagers to lift weights. Many, including doctors, parents, and coaches, thought it was dangerous, that it would cause injuries, stunt growth, and inhibit athletic performance. I actually had to lie to several of my coaches, and sneak in my weight training. I was doing it and seeing the results on a daily basis, so I could never figure out why they were against something that was helping me so much as an athlete. The bottom line was they just didn't know. There was very little information and research available.

My era was the first to really get involved in weight training, so it has take twenty years or so to see the long-term effects. Obviously it has not hurt me. Today, this dinosaur thinking is gone. We know better. Schools and corporations are adding weight training facilities. Everybody is getting involved with weight training. We all now know its good for us.

My 13-year-old son recently become in interested improving his basketball game and has been coming into our gym at home and watching me lift weights. He also began doing some exercises like leg presses, calf raises, and partial incline sit-ups. This has been great timing for the book because I have been able to see how well a 12- or 13-year-old can handle lifting weights. For the most part he does very well, but remember I am there supervising him and making sure he uses correct form, doesn't lift too much, and does not do exercises that are dangerous. With my help he is able to lift weights safely, but if I wasn't there this would not be the case.

Gray Area
If you research this subject, you will find limited material and some controversy surrounding the issue of preteens training with weights. If you ask the experts, they will hesitate to give you an answer and clear cut recommendation. This is a gray area, and nobody wants to stick their neck out. Nobody really has the answer. So this leaves us with the question of "What do we do with our preteens?" We obviously want them to be healthy, grow, and develop strong, in-shape bodies.

What is a Preteen?
If we are going to talk about preteens, it's best I define what I mean by preteen. They are those children between the ages of 10-12.

My Recommendations for Preteens
Based on my experience, I don't believe most preteens have the mental or physical maturity to engage in a serious weight training program. Although there are exceptions — those advanced in development (both physically and mentally) — across the board the majority of preteens are not ready for such serious physical activity.

However this does not mean I think they should sit in front of the TV all day playing video games. I think exercise is also critical for preteens, just not in the weight room. Weight training is serious business. It is a powerful and the most effective way to change your body.

So again, the question is, "what do you do with preteens?"

I like to see preteens involved in organized sports. I like to also see them doing an exercise program consisting of exercises like push-ups, and pull-ups, like I've outlined below.

My Favorite
Training Program for Preteens

Push-ups

Pull-ups

Body Squats

Partial Incline Sit-up

Crunch

Leg Raise

Hyperextensions

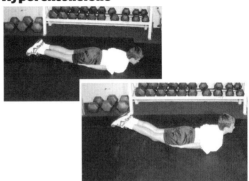

Training Routine
Monday, Wednesday, Friday

Sets of each exercise
10 years old - 1
11 years old - 2
12 years old - 3

Reps per exercise — Shoot for your age
10-10
11-11
12-12

Aerobic Exercise for Preteens
Aerobic exercise is a great way for preteens to exercise. Jogging, running, riding a stationary bike, and playing sports like soccer, basketball are great forms of exercise and will help preteens develop their bodies.

It's my opinion that if teens are going to train aerobically that they stay within the 20-30 minute time zone. Long aerobic workouts are not for preteens. They start to fatigue, lose form and technique, as well as lose mental focus after about 30 minutes. So I recommend 2-3 20-30 minute aerobic training sessions a week (keeping heart rate in the 70 percent range).

A Judgment Call
Everyone matures differently. Some preteens may have the mental and physical maturity to begin serious weight training, others may not. Some have the resources like well-supervised programs at school. I think it is best to stay a little on the conservative side. This is the beginning stages of maturity. Play it safe. Remember, there is a whole lifetime ahead to train. Better to start out on the right foot. Too much, too soon can cause problems later on down the road.

P a r t

Training For Sports

The goal for many who begin a training program is to enhance sports performance and to become a better athlete. This is a very good goal. I don't think there is anyone who wouldn't agree that a well-conditioned athlete is not a better athlete. Increases in strength, muscular size, power, flexibility, stamina, and endurance will enhance any athlete's ability to perform his or her sport more efficiently and effectively.

There is no doubt in my mind that a good training program would drastically improve your athletic performance. I've witnessed it with myself as well as with many others.

The better conditioned athlete is going to perform better — even with all other factors equal like skill level and age. They:

- don't get tired as easy
- conserve energy better
- perform sharper
- are more mentally alert
- are less likely to get injured
- recover form injuries quicker
- are more versatile
- have better agility
- are more confident

My Training for Sports

In the seven out of fourteen years I was involved in competitive sports, I trained using sports-specific training programs. For football I followed a football conditioning training program, for wrestling I followed a wrestling conditioning training program and likewise for track. I can tell you from my experience that a training program consisting of weight training, aerobic conditioning, and good nutritional practices will do more to improve skill and performance than anything else you could do. A well-conditioned athlete is by far a superior athlete.

My biggest athletic improvements and accomplishments always came after consistent pre-season, in-season, and post-season training programs. As a freshman in college, 6' tall and weighing 215 pounds, I would have never been able to walk on to a Division One program as a lineman, make the team, and eventually earn a scholarship had it not been for training intelligently using sports-specific training programs. My training programs allowed me to beat out players who were bigger, stronger, and faster, because I was a better conditioned athlete.

My Training Philosophy for All Athletes

Over the years I have been exposed to many coaches and with these coaches I have trained under many different training philosophies, as well as been exposed to various training techniques. I have trained under coaches who thought training with weights was bad and would slow you down. I have trained under coaches who thought all you had to do is train with weights, eat, and get bigger. I also trained under coaches who thought all you had to do was run, run, and run.

Looking back I would have to admit that many of these approaches were far off the mark. I have learned that training is not, as some have put it, adopting a few exercises, running a couple of miles, or taking a handful of vitamins. Training "intelligently" is a science of carefully calculated activities.

Training for twenty years has taught me that the best way to train for sports performance is to train a little like a power lifter, a little like a bodybuilder, a little like a sprinter, and a little like an endurance athlete. This equals total conditioning, resulting in a strong, powerful, toned, fit, healthy body that has plenty of strength, stamina, and endurance to perform.

The sports-specific training programs adopt this philosophy. They are constructed to give you exercises, routines, techniques, and guidelines to make you a better "overall" athlete.

Training for Sports

Training specifically for sports is a little different than training for general conditioning. A general conditioning program is designed to give you the basics of conditioning. However a sports-training program is designed to not only get you into shape, but to also develop skills that will help you to be able to perform better.

All sports are unique in their own way. They require different skills as well as different forms of conditioning. For instance, a shot putter needs powerful-strength both in the lower and upper body. Whereas a soccer player needs good leg strength plus aerobic stamina and endurance.

When training for sports improvement, its very important to know the specific skill requirements of that sport so you can intelligently organize a training program.

What follows in the next thirteen chapters are organized training programs for the most popular sports: football, hockey, baseball, basketball, track, golf, gymnastics, soccer, wrestling, tennis, volleyball, swimming, and extreme sports.

The Three Cycles of Training

For a training program to be effective, it needs to be set up into what are called training cycles — mini time periods of training.

Cycle One — Pre-season, "Hard Training Time"

This is when your training should take a top priority. You're getting ready for the upcoming season. This is the time you hold nothing back. The goal is to get into tip-top condition. Generally it means losing those fat pounds, increasing muscular body weight, strength, and power, as well as aerobic endurance, flexibility, and agility. It involves an intensive weight training and aerobic conditioning program.

Cycle Two — In-season "Maintenance"

Here, you work to maintain what was built in the pre-season. This program allows you to safely get you through the season, maintain strength levels, control body weight, and prevent injuries.

It is usually accomplished by training at minimal levels of weight training and aerobic conditioning. This is not a time to go all out and make up for a missed pre-season training program. This only leads to overtraining and burnout.

The season is a time to sharpen sports-specific skills, like tackling or shooting a basketball. The in-season training program is meant to work as a support program.

Cycle Three — Post-Season "Active Rest and Recovery"

This is a training cycle that is very seldom discussed or implemented. But one that I think is as important as the "pre-season" and "in-season" training cycles. I have found it to be vitality important both physically and mentally for the athlete.

Generally this is a time to rehabilitate injuries, cycle down from hard training, get rest, and let the body recover. Quitting cold turkey in my opinion is not wise; it often leads to weight gain and deconditioning, depression, and lethargy. It also increases the time necessary to recover from injuries. This approach usually leads to an athlete getting really out of shape, and this always makes it harder both mentally and physically to get the "engine" started again when the new season rolls around. As a matter a fact, the engine is a good analogy — the less you drive a car, the harder it is to start, and the less likely it will run at top performance.

When I abruptly took long lengths of time off from the weight room, running track, etc., I gained weight, had loads of muscles aches and pains, and felt depressed. It made it very hard to get myself motivated to train again when the new season approached, particularly because I was physically out of shape. Mentally I was lethargic, unmotivated, and unfocused.

In the post-season there is a delicate balance between R & R and physical activity. It does not mean that you should sit on the couch, play video games, and eat chocolate sundaes. Nor does it mean running marathons and lifting tons of weights.

It means implementing an active rest and recovery post-season training program.

Successful Sports-Specific Training Programs
A successful training program should:
- ♦ Get you into top performance condition
- ♦ Help you perform the skills of your sport better
- ♦ Increase your confidence
- ♦ Sharpen your mind and challenge you to strive toward new levels of achievement

A successful training program needs purpose, planning, organization, careful calculation, continual adjustments, consistent attention, and intelligent execution.

Please keep in mind that sports training is not an exact science. We are discovering and learning every day. Although certain principles apply to all training routines and techniques, you won't find two trainers, coaches, or authors in total agreement on everything. There simply is more than one way to skin the cat.

What I have outlined for you in the next thirteen chapters are my favorite sports training techniques and routines based on my personal training experience and beliefs. It is not intended to replace a well-structured and supervised program at your school.

However, if you are in a school sponsored program, you may wish to adopt the pre-season and post-season training programs (very few schools have the resources to train athletes year round).

Take as much information as you can and adapt it to a training program to fit your needs. Then watch it supercharge your sports performance!

Training for Football

12

Football is a sport where power, size, speed, strength, agility, and endurance make a big difference. If you are going to be a good football player, then you are going to have to get involved in a serious conditioning program of weight training and aerobic conditioning. All the movements in football, require explosive strength, and explosive strength is best developed through weight training.

Playing competitive football for eleven years I have learned one thing clearly: To be a good football player you need strength and aerobic conditioning aimed at overall muscular development and balance.Getting involved in a good pre-season, in-season, and post-season training program will give a player the mental and physical advantage that is necessary to excel and provide the winning advantage.

My Favorite
Training Programs for Football

Pre-season Football Training

Pre-season football training is a very important training cycle for the athlete. Lifting weights and conditioning the cardiovascular system will prepare your body for the physical demands that the season will require. Pre-season football training is a time to focus on developing a good foundation of size, strength, endurance, flexibility, and explosive power.

This is best accomplished in the weight room by doing basic compound exercises such as bench presses, squats, and power cleans — exercises that put an emphasis on major muscle groups of the legs, chest, and back. I also recommend special attention for the shoulders, incorporating specific should exercises such as dumbbell lateral raises to the front and side. (Shoulders take a pounding in football.)

Pre-season Training Routine

Monday, Tuesday, Thursday, Friday
Monday — Heavy Upper Body
chest, back, shoulders, biceps,triceps, neck, abs

Tuesday — Heavy Lower Body
quadriceps, hamstrings, calves, lower back, abs

Thursday — Light Upper Body
chest, back, shoulders, biceps,triceps, neck, abs

Friday — Light Lower Body
quadriceps, hamstrings, calves, lower back, abs

Monday/Thursday — Upper Body

**Smith Machine
Chest Press**

**Incline
Dumbbell Press**

**Lat Pulldown
(behind the
neck)**

Training for Football

Pre-season

T
r
a
i
For
n
i
F
n
o
g
o
t
b
a
l
l

Low Pulley Cable Row

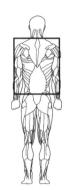

Smith Machine Shoulder Press (front of neck)

Dumbbell Lateral Raise

Dumbbell Front Raise

Barbell Arm Curl

Bench Dips

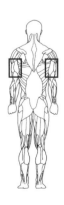

Training for Football

Pre-season

Training For Football

4-Way Neck Isometrics

Partial Incline Sit-Up

Hanging Leg Raise

138

Pre-season

Barbell Power Clean

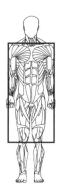

Leg Press

Smith Machine Squat

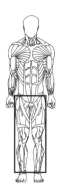

Training for Football

Pre-season

T r a i n i n g

For

F o o t b a l l

Leg Extension

Lying Leg Curl

Smith Machine Standing Calf Raise

Pre-season

Crunch

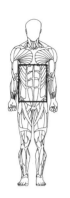  

Knee-ups Incline Bench

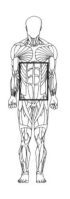 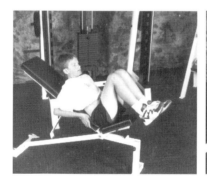 

Hyperextension

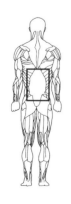  

Pre-season

Pre-season Sets & Reps
Monday/Tuesday — Heavy Day
3 sets of each exercise: 1st set 10 reps, 2nd set 8 reps, 3rd set 6 reps

Thursday/Friday — Light Day
2 sets of each exercise: 1st set 12 reps, 2nd set 8 reps

Pre-season Poundages
All Upper Body Exercises
Increase weight 5-10 pounds per set

Lower Body Exercises — Leg Press, Squat, Calf Raise
Increase weight 10-20 pounds per set

Leg Extension and Leg Curl
Increase weight 5-10 pounds per set

Nonweight Assisted Exercises — Neck Iso, Abdominals, Hyperextensions
Exercise to failure

Pre-season Rest Between Sets
2 minutes

Pre-season Techniques
Pyramid — Increase the weight for each set while at the same time decreasing the number of reps you perform. This is the best technique for building muscle mass as well as developing strength and explosive power.

Pre-season Aerobic Training
Three times per week:
Workout 1   Jog 40 minutes
Workout 2   Run 20 minutes (hustle pace)
Workout 3   Sprints:
1 220 yd. full stride
2 100 yd. dashes
2 60 yd. dashes
2 40 yd. dashes
2 20 yd. dashes
2 10 yd. dashes

Pre-season Stretching
Full body stretch after all weight training and aerobic sessions. (See Chapter 26 for key body stretches.)

My Favorite

Training Programs for Football

In-Season Training

A big mistake that many athletes make is training very hard during the pre-season and not training during the season to maintain what the level of fitness they established prior to the beginning of the season. In-season training will do just that. It is a program to maintain the conditioning levels built up in the off-season, as well as preventive medicine for most injuries. Let me caution you: in-season training is not a time to take risks in the weight room. In-season training involves training with weights, at a minimum level — just enough to maintain conditioning levels.

In-season Training Routine

Monday, Thursday
Monday/Lower Body
quadriceps, hamstrings, calves, lower back, abs, neck

Thursday/Upper Body
chest, back, shoulders, biceps, triceps, neck, abs

Training For Football

In-season

Monday

Leg Press

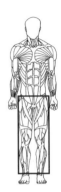

Leg Extension

Leg Curl

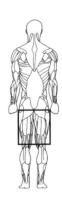

Smith Machine Standing Calf Raise

Crunch

Knee-ups Incline Bench

Training for Football

In-season

Training For Football

In-season

Hyperextension

 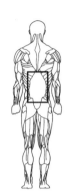

4-Way Neck Iso's

Thursday

Smith Machine Chest Press

Lat Pulldown Wide Grip (behind the neck)

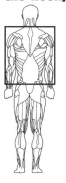

Seated Low Row

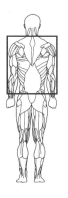

Smith Machine Shoulder Press (front of neck)

In-season

Training

For Football

Dumbbell Lateral Raise

Barbell Arm Curl

Bench Dips

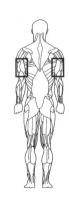

In-season

Partial Incline Sit-up

Hanging Leg Raise

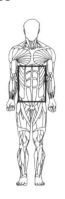

Training

for

Football

149

Pre-season

In-season Sets & Reps
Monday/Thursday — 2 sets of each exercise
1st set 10 reps, 2nd set 8 reps

In-season Poundages
All Upper Body Exercises
Increase weight 5-10 pounds per set

Lower Body Exercises — Leg Press, Squat, Calf Raise
Increase weight 10-20 pounds per set

Leg Extension and Leg Curl
Increase weight 5-10 pounds per set

Nonweight Assisted Exercises — Neck Iso, Abdominals, Hyperextensions
Exercise to failure

In-season Rest Between Sets
1-2 minutes

In-season Techniques
Pyramid— Increase the weight for each set while at the same time decreasing the number of reps you perform. This is the best technique for building muscle mass as well as developing strength and explosive power.

In-season Aerobic Training
None

In-season Stretching
Full body stretch after all weight training and aerobic sessions. (See Chapter 26 for key body stretches.)

For post-season Football training program see the All Sports Post Season Training Program section on page 353.

13 Training for Hockey

Several years ago I bought a pair of roller blades and started playing around with a hockey stick and a puck. After several scrapes and bruises, I was gliding around the pavement moving with precision and grace. I remember thinking "Boy, hockey is a fun sport, and how I wish it had been around when I was in school." Hockey is a sport for tough athletes; it is a fast-paced, multifaceted game that requires speed, strength, agility, flexibility, endurance, balance, and toughness.

In 1995, my good friend Steve Hoffacker and I became sponsors for a professional hockey team. We donated several thousand dollars worth of weight training machines to the organization to set up a training facility in the coliseum for the players. After watching several games since then, I am sure that the training is paying great dividends for the players and the organization.

My Favorite
Training Programs for Hockey

Pre-season Training

Pre-season hockey training is a very important training cycle for the athlete. Lifting weights and conditioning the cardiovascular system will prepare your body for the physical demands that the season will require. It is a time to focuse on developing a good foundation of size, strenght, endurance, flexibility, and explosive power.

This is best accomplished in the weight room by doing basic compound exercises such as bench presses, squats, and power cleans (exercises that put emphasis on the major muscle groups of the legs, chest and back). I also recommend special attention for the shoulders, incorporating specific exercises such as dumbbell lateral raises to the front and side since the shoulders take a pounding in this sport. Also include some specialized leg training exercises like lunges and step-ups.

Pre-season Training Routine

Monday, Wednesday, Friday
Monday — Upper Body
chest, shoulders, triceps, abs

Wednesday — Lower Body
quadriceps, hamstrings, calves, lower back, abs

Friday — Upper Body
back, biceps, forearms, neck, abs

Smith Machine Bench Press

Incline Dumbbell Press

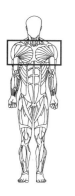

Smith Machine Shoulder Press

Training for Hockey

Pre-season

Kris Gebhardt

Training

For

Hockey

Dumbbell Lateral Raise

Dumbbell Front Raise

Tricep Cable Pushdown

Pre-season

154

Partial Incline Sit-up

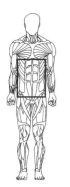

Hanging Leg Raise

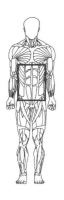

Wednesday — Lower Body

Barbell Power Clean

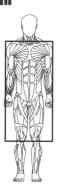

Training for Hockey

Pre-season

Training For Hockey

Leg Press

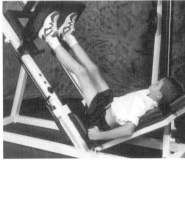 

Smith Machine Squat

Smith Machine Lunge

Pre-season

Leg Extension

Leg Curl

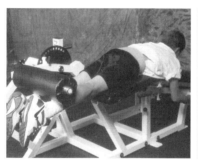

Smith Machine Standing Calf Raise

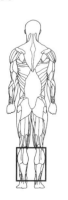

Pre-season

T r a i n i n g
for
H o c k e y

Seated Calf Machine

Crunch

Knee-ups Incline Bench

Hyperextension

Friday — Upper Body

**Lat Pulldown
Wide Grip
(behind the neck)**

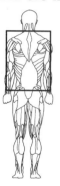

**Low Pulley
Cable Row**

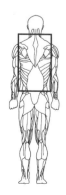

Training for Hockey

Pre-season

Training For Hockey

Face Down Incline Dumbbell Row

Barbell Arm Curl

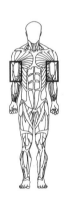

Low Pulley Curl

Pre-season

160

Barbell Wrist Curl

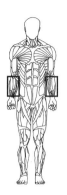

4-Way Neck Machine

Cable Crunch

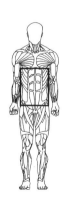

Training for Hockey

Pre-season

Pre-season Sets & Reps
Monday/Wednesday/Friday — 3 sets of each exercise
1st set 10 reps, 2nd set 8 reps, 3rd set 6 reps

Pre-season Poundages
All Upper Body Exercises
Increase weight 5-10 pounds per set

Lower Body Exercises — Leg Press, Squat, Calf Raise
Increase weight 10-20 pounds per set

Leg Extension and Leg Curl
Increase weight 5-10 pounds per set

Nonweight Assisted Exercises — Neck Iso, Abdominals, Hyperextensions
Exercise to Failure

Pre-season Rest Between Sets
2 minutes

Pre-season Techniques
Pyramid — Increase the weight for each set while decreasing the number of reps you perform. This is the best technique for building muscle mass, developing strength, and explosive power.

Pre-season Aerobic Training (three times per week)
Workout 1   Jog 40 minutes
Workout 2   Run 20 minutes (hustle pace)
Workout 3   Sprints:
1 220 yd. full stride
2 100 yd. dashes
2 60 yd. dashes
2 40 yd. dashes
2 20 yd. dashes
2 10 yd. dashes

Pre-season Stretching
Full body stretch after all weight training and aerobic sessions. (See Chapter 26 for key body stretches.)

My Favorite
Training Programs for Hockey

In-Season Training

The hockey season is long and physically demanding. A big mistake that many athletes make is training very hard during the pre-season and not training during the season to maintain the level of fitness they have built up. In-season straining is just that, a maintentance program to maintain the condition levels built in the off-season. It is also a good way to prevent injuries and also to heal injuries that may occur during the season.

Let me caution you: In-season training is not the time to take risks in the weight room. In-season training involves training with weights at a minimum level — just enough to maintain conditioning levels.

In-season Training Routine

Monday/Thursday
Whole Body
chest, back, shoulders, biceps, triceps, quadriceps, hamstrings, calves, lower back, abs

Smith Machine Bench Press

Lat Pulldown Wide Grip (behind the neck)

Smith Machine Shoulder Press (front of the neck)

In-season

Barbell Arm Curl

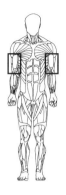

Tricep Cable Pushdown

Leg Press

Training for Hockey

In-season

Training For Hockey

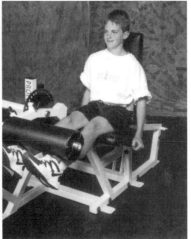

Leg Extension

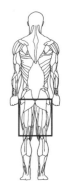

Leg Curl

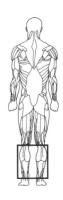

Smith Machine Standing Calf Raise

In-season

166

Crunch

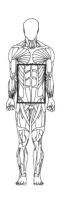

Hanging Leg Raises

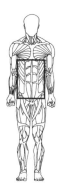

Hyperextension

Training for Hockey

In-season

**4-Way Neck
Iso's (work once
a week)**

Training

For Hockey

In-season Sets & Reps
Monday/Thursday — 2 sets of each exercise
1st set 10 reps, 2nd set 8 reps

In-season Poundages
All Upper Body Exercise
Increase weight 5-10 pounds per set

Lower Body Exercise — Leg Press, Squat, Calf Raise
Increase weight 10-20 pounds per set

Leg Extension and Leg Curl
Increase weight 5-10 pounds per set

Nonweight Assisted Exercise — Neck Iso, Abdominals, Hyperextensions
Exercise to failure

In-season Rest Between Sets
1-2 minutes

In-season Techniques
Pyramid — Increase the weight for each set while decreasing the number of reps you perform. This is the best technique for building muscle mass, developing strength, and explosive power.

In-season Aerobic Training
None

In-season Stretching
Full body stretch after all weight training and aerobic sessions. (See Chapter 26 for key body stretches.)

For post-season Hockey training program see the All Sports Post Season Training Program section on page 353.

Training for Baseball

Between 1985 and 1989, I spent quite a bit of time in the locker room of the Detroit Tigers professional baseball team. I remember how shocked I was at discovering that very few of the players participated in any form of weight training. The few that did would scurry off after practice to some dark, dingy room in the basement of the coliseum, and train on makeshift benches with plastic, cement-filled weights. I remember thinking how can professionals, the very elite athletes of the sport not be training to improve their performance, protect themselves from injury, and get themselves into the best possible shape?

I discussed this with the president of the organization at dinner one night. His response was that most of the coaches frown on weight training. He said, they thought it would make the players muscle bound, slow them down, and cause them to lose the mechanics of their swing. I remember arguing that this was a very archaic and limited point of view. But my words fell on deaf ears.

The other day I happen to turn on ESPN.

They were running a special on the merits of weight training for the baseball player. It seems that the professional baseball teams have caught up with the times and are implementing weight training programs for their players. The organizations are even footing the bill and installing state-of-the-art facilities. Several of the players were interviewed and admitted that the weight training did not slow them down, but in fact made them faster. It also gave them more power; helped them recover more quickly from games; and for many, helped them extend the length of their careers.

Baseball players, like other athletes need to be in good shape; the sport requires good upper and lower body strength and flexibility, as well as muscular and aerobic endurance. Weight training for baseball players is indeed here to stay! A good year-round training program will do a lot to enhance your game.

Training Programs for Baseball

Pre-season Training

Pre-season baseball training is a very important training cycle for the athlete. Lifting weights and conditioning the cardiovascular system will prepare your body for the physical demands that the season will require. It is a time to focus on developing a good foundation of strength, endurance, flexibility, and power.

This is best accomplished in the weight room by doing basic compound exercises such as bench presses, shoulder presses, and leg presses (exercises that put emphasis on the major muscle groups of the legs, chest and back). I also recommend special attention for the shoulders, incorporating specific exercises such as dumbbell lateral raises for the side of the shoulder.

Pre-season Training Routine

Monday, Wednesday, Friday
Monday — Upper Body
chest, shoulders, triceps, abs

Wednesday — Lower Body
quadriceps, hamstrings, calves, lower back, abs

Friday — Upper Body
back, biceps, forearms, neck, abs

Monday — Upper Body

Smith Machine Bench Press

Incline Dumbbell Press

Smith Machine Shoulder Press

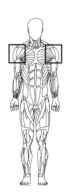

Training for Baseball

Pre-season

T r a i n i n g

for

B a s e b a l l

Dumbbell Lateral Raise

Tricep Cable Pushdown

Partial Incline Sit-up

Pre-season

Leg Raise

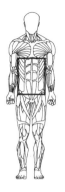

Wednesday — Lower Body

Leg Press

Smith Machine Squat

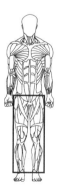

175

Training for Baseball

Pre-season

Leg Extension

Leg Curl

Smith Machine Standing Calf Raise

Training for Baseball

Pre-season

Seated Calf Machine

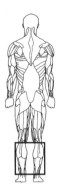  

Crunch

Knee-ups Incline Bench

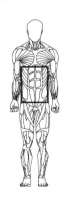  

Training for Baseball

Pre-season

Training for Baseball

for

Pre-season

Hyperextension

  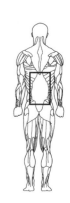

Lat Pulldown Wide Grip (behind the neck)

Low Pulley Cable Row

   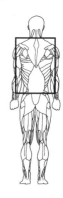

Facedown Incline Dumbbell Row

Barbell Arm Curl

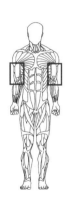

Reverse Barbell Curl

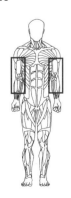

Training for Baseball

Pre-season

Training for Baseball

Barbell Wrist Curl

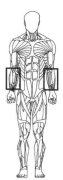

Pre-season

180

Pre-season Sets & Reps
Monday/Wednesday/Friday — 3 sets of each exercise
1st set 10 reps, 2nd set 8 reps 3rd set 6 reps

Pre-season Poundages
All Upper Body Exercises
Increase weight 5-10 pounds per set

Lower Body Exercises — Leg Press, Squat, Calf Raise
Increase weight 10-20 pounds per set

Leg Extension and Leg Curl
Increase weight 5-10 pounds per set

Nonweight Assisted Exercises — Neck Iso, Abdominals, Hyperextensions
Exercise to Failure

Pre-season Rest Between Sets
2 minutes

Pre-season Techniques
Pyramid — Increase the weight for each set while decreasing the number of reps you perform. This is the best technique for building muscle mass, developing strength, and explosive power.

Pre-season Aerobic Training (Three times per week)
Workout 1 Jog 40 minutes
Workout 2 Run 20 minutes (hustle pace)
Workout 3 Sprints:
1 220 yd. full stride
2 100 yd. dashes
2 60 yd. dashes
2 40 yd. dashes
2 20 yd. dashes
2 10 yd. dashes

Pre-season Stretching
Full body stretch after all weight training and aerobic sessions. (See Chapter 26 for key body stretches.)

My Favorite

Training Programs for Baseball

In-Season Training

Baseball players play a lot of games, with games on weekends, during the week, tournaments, and doubleheaders. The season can get long and tiresome. It's important to keep this in mind when continuing your training program throughout the season. It's very easy with all the practice, games, and training to overtrain. I like to advise baseball players to train twice a week with weights during the season. This seems to be enough to maintain the conditioning levels achieved in pre-season training, prevent injuries, and speed recovery if injuries do occur. And in most cases, you won't overtrain with a twice a week routine.

In-season Training Routine

Monday/Thursday
Whole Body
chest, back, shoulders, biceps, triceps, quadriceps, hamstrings, calves, lower back, abs

**Smith Machine
Bench Press**

**Lat Pulldown
Wide Grip
(behind the neck)**

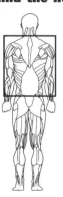

**Smith Machine
Shoulder Press
(front of the
neck)**

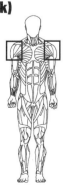

Training for Baseball

In-season

Training

For Baseball

Barbell Arm Curl

Barbell Wrist Curl

Tricep Cable Pushdown

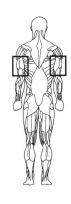

Leg Press

Leg Extension

Leg Curl

Training for Baseball

In-season

Training For Baseball

Smith Machine Standing Calf Raise

Crunch

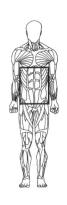

Hanging Leg Raises

In-season

Hyperextension

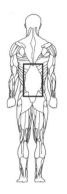  

Training for Baseball

In-season

In-season Sets & Reps
Monday/Thursday — 2 sets of each exercise
1st set 10 reps. 2nd set 8 reps

In-season Poundages
All Upper Body Exercise
Increase weight 5-10 pounds per set

Lower Body Exercise — Leg Press, Squat, Calf Raise
Increase weight 10-20 pounds per set

Leg Extension and Leg Curl
Increase weight 5-10 pounds per set

Nonweight Assisted Exercise — Neck Iso, Abdominals, Hyperextensions
Exercise to failure

In-season Rest Between Sets
1-2 minutes

In-season Techniques
Pyramid — Increase the weight for each set while decreasing the number
of reps you perform. This is the best technique for building muscle mass,
developing strength, and explosive power.

In-season Aerobic Training
None

In-season Stretching
Full body stretch after all weight training and aerobic sessions. (See Chapter
26 for key body stretches.)

Special Notes for In-season Training
Depending on game schedule, you may need to adjust weight training
days. For example, if you have a game on Thursday night, move Thursday's
weight training session to Friday.

For post-season baseball training program see the All Sports Post Season
Training Program section on page 353.

15

Training for Basketball

I want to dispel some myths about training with weights as a basketball player. Number one: lifting weights properly will not cause you to become inflexible. As a matter of fact, lifting weights properly will increase your overall flexibility. Number two: lifting weights will not slow you down. It will develop explosive power, agility, speed, and quickness. Number three: lifting weights will not throw your shot off.

As a basketball player your goals are the same as any other athlete — to improve performance. Like in other sports, this is accomplished by becoming a better conditioned athlete.

Participating in a good year-round training program will help you gain muscle mass, lose body fat, increase strength, power, flexibility, and agility. You will also tone your muscles, increase muscular endurance, and give yourself the mental edge needed to be a peak performing athlete.

Basketball is not a passive sport. It's a

physical game that requires a combination of good physical development and mental toughness. The following pre-season and in-season training programs will provide you with the exercises and training guidelines to elevate your game to the next level.

My Favorite
Training Programs for Basketball

Pre-season Basketball

Pre-season basketball training is a very important training cycle for the athlete. Lifting weights and conditioning the cardiovascular system will prepare your body for the physical demands that the season will require. It is a time to focus on developing a good foundation of size, strength, endurance, flexibility, and explosive power.

This is best accomplished in the weight room by doing basic compound exercises such as bench presses, squats, and power cleans (exercises that put emphasis on the major muscle groups of the legs, chest and back). I also recommend special attention for the legs, incorporating exercises such as step-ups and seated calf raises.

Pre-season Training Routine

Monday, Wednesday, Friday
Monday — Upper Body
chest, shoulders, triceps, abs

Wednesday — Lower Body
quadriceps, hamstrings, calves, lower back, abs

Friday — Light Upper Body
back, biceps, forearms, abs

Monday — Upper Body

**Smith Machine
Bench Press**

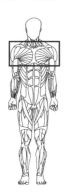

**Incline
Dumbbell Press**

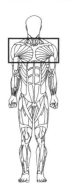

**Smith Machine
Shoulder Press
(front of the
neck)**

Training for Basketball

Pre-season

Training

Dumbbell Lateral Raise

Smith Machine Close Grip Press

Partial Incline Sit-up

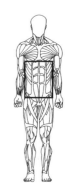

Pre-season

Hanging Leg Raise

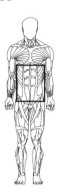

Wednesday — Lower Body

Barbell Power Clean

Leg Press

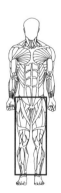

Training for Basketball

193

Pre-season

Training For Basketball

Pre-season

Smith Machine Squat

Dumbbell Step Ups

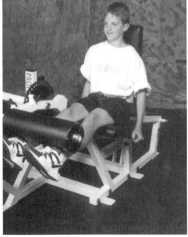

Leg Extension

Lying Leg Curl

Smith Machine Standing Calf Raise

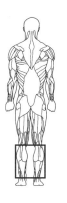  

Seated Calf Machine

Training for Basketball

Pre-season

T r a i n i n g

For

B a s k e t b a l l

Crunch

Knee-ups Incline Bench

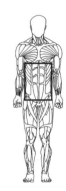

Hyperextension

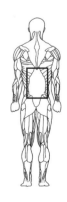

Pre-season

Friday — Upper Body

Lat Pulldown Wide Grip (behind the neck)

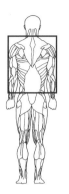

Low Pulley Cable Row

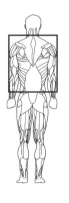

One Arm Dumbbell Row

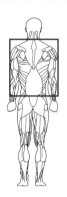

Training for Basketball

Pre-season

Training For Basketball

Barbell Arm Curl

 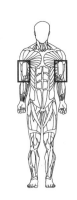

Hammer Dumbbell Curl

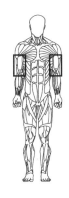

Barbell Wrist Curls

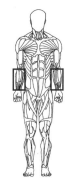

Pre-season

Cable Crunch

Training for Basketball

Pre-season

Pre-season Sets & Reps
Monday/Wednesday/Friday — 3 sets of each exercise
1st set 10 reps, 2nd set 8 reps, 3rd set 6 reps

Pre-season Poundages
All Upper Body Exercises
Increase weight 5-10 pounds per set

Lower Body Exercises — Leg Press, Squat, Calf Raise
Increase weight 10-20 pounds per set

Leg Extension and Leg Curl
Increase weight 5-10 pounds per set

Nonweight Assisted Exercises — Neck Iso, Abdominals, Hyperextensions
Exercise to Failure

Pre-season Rest Between Sets
2 minutes

Pre-season Techniques
Pyramid — Increase the weight for each set while decreasing the number of reps you perform. This is the best technique for building muscle mass, developing strength, and explosive power.

Pre-season Aerobic Training (three times per week)
Workout 1 Jog 40 minutes
Workout 2 Run 20 minutes (hustle pace)
Workout 3 Sprints:
1 220 yd. full stride
2 100 yd. dashes
2 60 yd. dashes
2 40 yd. dashes
2 20 yd. dashes
2 10 yd. dashes

Pre-season Stretching
Full body stretch after all weight training and aerobic sessions. (See Chapter 26 for key body stretches.)

My Favorite
Training Programs for Basketball

In-Season Training

Basketball players play a lot of games, with games on weekends, during the week, and tournaments. The season can get long and tiresome. It's important to keep this in mind when continuing your training program throughout the season. It's very easy with all the practice, games, and training to overtrain. I like to advise basketball players to train twice a week with weights during the season. This seems to be enough to maintain the conditioning levels achieved in pre-season training, prevent injuries, and speed recovery if injuries do occur.

In-season Training Routine

Monday/Thursday — Whole Body
chest, back, shoulders, biceps, triceps, quadriceps, hamstrings, calves, lower back, abs

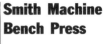

Training

For

Basketball

Smith Machine Bench Press

Lat Pulldown Wide Grip (behind the neck)

Smith Machine Shoulder Press (front of the neck)

Barbell Arm Curl

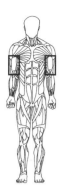

Tricep Cable Pushdown

Leg Press

Training for Basketball

In-season

Training For Basketball

Leg Extension

Leg Curl

Smith Machine Standing Calf Raise

In-season

Crunch

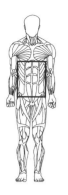

Incline Bench Knee-ups

Hyperextension

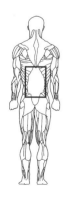

Training for Basketball

In-season

In-season Poundages
Monday/Thursday — 2 sets of each exercise
1st set 10 reps, 2nd set 8 reps

In-season Poundages
All Upper Body Exercise
Increase weight 5-10 pounds per set

Lower Body Exercise — Leg Press, Squat, Calf Raise
Increase weight 10-20 pounds per set

Leg Extension and Leg Curl
Increase weight 5-10 pounds per set

Nonweight Assisted Exercise: Abdominals, Hyperextensions
Exercise to failure

In-season Rest Between
Sets 1-2 minutes

In-season Techniques
Pyramid — Increase the weight for each set while decreasing the number of reps you perform. This is the best technique for building muscle mass, developing strength, and explosive power.

In-season Aerobic Training
None

In-season Stretching
Full body stretch after all weight training and aerobic sessions. (See Chapter 26 for key body stretches.)

Special Notes for In-season Training
Depending on game schedule, you may need to adjust weight training days. For example, if you have a game on Thursday night, move Thursday's weight training session to Friday.

For post-season basketball training program see the All Sports Post Season Training Program section on page 353.

Training for
Cross Country

Cross country is a sport that is aerobically demanding. Running for or five miles or more a day is quite a challenge. Yet, while running really gets the cardiovascular system into good shape, it does little for the muscles of the body.

The demands of intensive running add up as the season progresses, and many runners experience fatigue, weight loss, weakness, injuries, aches, and pains. Participating in a good pre-season and in-season training program which incorporates weights is a great way to ward off the negative effects of running miles and miles every day.

Few runners lack aerobic conditioning or are concerned with losing weight. The big concern for most runners is increasing and maintaining strength and muscle mass.

My Favorite

Training Programs for Cross Country

Pre-season Training

Pre-season cross country training is a very important training cycle for the athlete. Lifting weights and conditioning the cardiovascular system will prepare your body for the physical demands that the season will require. It is a time to focus on developing a good foundation of strength, endurance, and flexibility.

This is best accomplished in the weight room by doing basic compound exercises such as bench presses, leg presses, and shoulder presses (exercises that put emphasis on the major muscle groups of the legs, chest and back).

Pre-season Training Routine

Monday, Wednesday, Friday
Monday — Upper Body
chest, shoulders, triceps, abs

Wednesday — Lower Body
quadriceps, hamstrings, calves, lower back, abs

Friday — Upper Body
back, biceps, forearms, abs

Monday — Upper Body

Smith Machine Bench Press

Incline Dumbbell Press

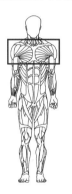

Smith Machine Shoulder Press (front of the neck)

Training for Cross Country

Pre-season

Training

For

Cross Country

Smith Machine Upright Row

Bench Dips

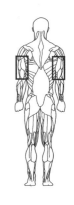

Broomstick Twists

Pre-season

Partial Incline Sit-up

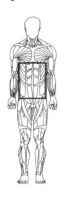

Incline Bench Knee-ups

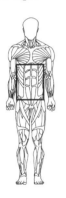

Wednesday — Lower Body

Leg Press

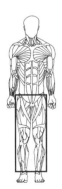

Pre-season

Training for Cross Country

Training for Cross Country

Smith Machine Squat

 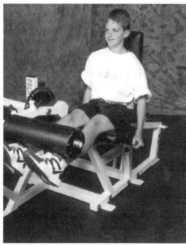 

Leg Extension

Lying Leg Curl

  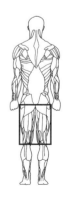

Pre-season

Smith Machine Standing Calf Raise

Seated Calf Machine

Reverse Crunch

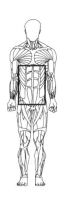

Training For Cross Country

Pre-season

Training For Cross Country

Knee-ups Incline Bench

Hyperextension

Friday — Upper Body

Lat Pulldown Wide Grip (behind the neck)

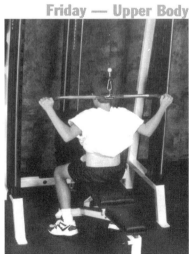

Low Pulley Cable Row

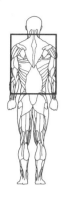

One Arm Dumbbell Row

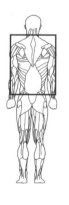

Two Arm Dumbbell Curl

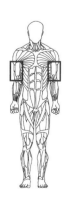

215

Pre-season

Low Pulley Arm Curl

Pre-season

Pre-season Sets & Reps
Monday/Wednesday/Friday — 3 sets of each exercise
1st set 10 reps, 2nd set 8 reps, 3rd set 6 reps

Pre-season Poundages
All Upper Body Exercises
Increase weight 5-10 pounds per set

Lower Body Exercises — Leg Press, Squat, Calf Raise
Increase weight 10-20 pounds per set

Leg Extension and Leg Curl
Increase weight 5-10 pounds per set

Nonweight Assisted Exercises — Abdominals, Hyperextensions
Exercise to Failure

Pre-season Rest Between Sets
2 minutes

Pre-season Techniques
Pyramid — Increase the weight for each set while decreasing the number of reps you perform. This is the best technique for building muscle mass, developing strength, and explosive power.

Pre-season Aerobic Training
Follow normal off-season running program

Pre-season Stretching
Full body stretch after all weight training and aerobic sessions. (See Chapter 26 for key body stretches.)

My Favorite
Training Programs for Cross Country

In-Season Training

Cross country runners run a lot of miles. The season can get long and tiresome. It's important to keep this in mind when continuing your training program throughout the season. It's very easy with all the practice, games, and training to overtrain. I like to advise cross country runners to train twice a week with weights during the season. This seems to be enough to maintain the conditioning levels achieved in pre-season training, prevent injuries, and speed recovery if injuries do occur.

In-season Training Routine

Monday/Thursday – Whole Body
chest, back, shoulders, biceps, triceps, quadriceps, hamstrings, calves, lower back, abs

Smith Machine Bench Press

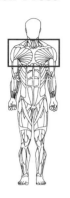

Lat Pulldown Wide Grip (behind the neck)

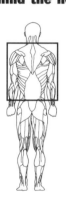

Smith Machine Shoulder Press (front of the neck)

Training For Cross Country

In-season

Training For Cross Country

Barbell Arm Curl

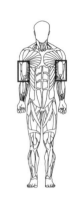

Tricep Cable Pushdown

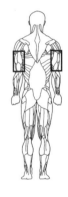

Leg Press

In-season

Leg Extension

Lying Leg Curl

Smith Machine Standing Calf Raise

221

In-season

Training For Cross Country

Broomstick Twists

Crunch

Incline Bench Knee-ups

In-season

Hyperextension

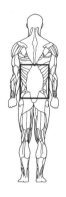 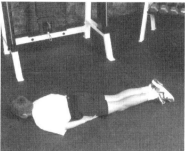 

In-season

In-season Sets & Reps
Monday/Thursday — 2 sets of each exercise
1st set 10 reps, 2nd set 8 reps

In-season Poundages
All Upper Body Exercise
Increase weight 5-10 pounds per set

Lower Body Exercise — Leg Press, Squat, Calf Raise
Increase weight 10-20 pounds per set

Leg Extension and Leg Curl
Increase weight 5-10 pounds per set

Nonweight Assisted Exercise: Abdominals, Hyperextensions
Exercise to failure

In-season Rest Between Sets
1-2 minutes

In-season Techniques
Pyramid — Increase the weight for each set while decreasing the number of reps you perform. This is the best technique for building muscle mass, developing strength, and explosive power.

In-season Aerobic Training
None

In-season Stretching
Full body stretch after all weight training and aerobic sessions. (See Chapter 26 for key body stretches.)

Special Notes for In-season Training
Depending on meet schedule, you may need to adjust weight training days. For example, if you have a meet on Thursday night, move Thursday's weight training session to Friday.

For post-season cross country training program see the All Sports Post Season Training Program section on page 353.

Training for Golf

When I worked for a specialty fitness equipment superstore, golfers would almost on a daily basis come into the store looking for the latest miracle piece of equipment to improve their swing. Usually it was some apparatus that they saw advertised on late night TV. You've seen the products — miracle stretch rubber bands, the forearm flexomatic — all advertised to be the answer to improving your golf swing and driving the ball further down the green.

The mechanics of a golf swing require more than just the muscles in your forearms. It involves almost every major muscle group in the body, from the calves to your lower back and abdominals, and also your shoulders and neck. Many muscles are involved in the swinging of a club.

Golfers who want to improve their swing, as well as every aspect of their game will do best by getting involved in an overall body training and conditioning program. As in all sports, a stronger, in-shape, well-conditioned athlete will perform better.

Although golf is not a physically demanding sport, being in good shape will do a tremendous amount to improve your performance.

My Favorite
Training Programs for Golf

Pre-season Training

Pre-season golf training is a very important training cycle for the athlete. Lifting weights and conditioning the cardiovascular system will prepare your body for the season. It is a time to focus on developing a good foundation of strength, endurance, flexibility, and explosive power.

This is best accomplished in the weight room by doing basic compound exercises such as bench presses, shoulder presses, and leg presses (exercises that put emphasis on the major muscle groups of the legs, chest and back). I also recommend special exercises for the lower back and abdominals.

Pre-season Training Routine

Monday, Wednesday, Friday
Monday — Upper Body
chest, shoulders, triceps, abs

Wednesday — Lower Body
quadriceps, hamstrings, calves, lower back, abs

Friday — Upper Body
back, biceps, forearms, abs

Smith Machine Bench Press

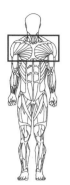

Incline Dumbbell Press

Smith Machine Shoulder Press (front of the neck)

Training for Golf

227

Pre-season

Training For Golf

Dumbbell Lateral Raise

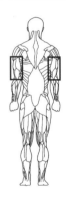

Overhead Dumb-bell Extension

Broomstick Twists

Partial Incline Sit-up

Hanging Leg Raise

Wednesday — Lower Body

Leg Press

229

Pre-season

Training for Golf

Dumbbell Squat

Leg Extension

 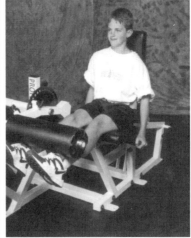

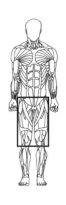

Leg Curl

Smith Machine Standing Calf Raise

Calf Raise on Leg Press

Crunch

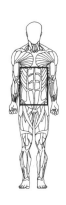

231

T
r
a
i
n
i
n
g

For
G
o
l
f

Knee-ups Incline Bench

  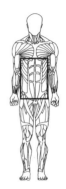

Hyperextension

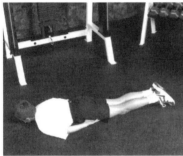  

Friday — Upper Body

Lat Pulldown Wide Grip (behind the neck)

  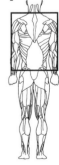

Pre-season

Low Pulley Cable Row

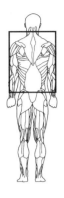

Stiff Arm Pulldown

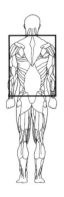

Two Arm Dumbbell Curl

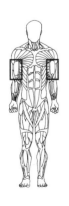

Pre-season

Training

Hammer Dumbbell Curl

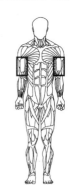

Barbell Wrist Curls

for Golf

Pre-season Sets & Reps
Monday/Wednesday/Friday — 3 sets of each exercise
1st set 10 reps, 2nd set 8 reps, 3rd set 6 reps

Pre-season Poundages
All Upper Body Exercises
Increase weight 5-10 pounds per set

Lower Body Exercises — Leg Press, Squat, Calf Raise
Increase weight 10-20 pounds per set

Leg Extension and Leg Curl
Increase weight 10-20 pounds per set

Nonweight Assisted Exercises — Abdominals, Hyperextensions
Exercise to Failure

Pre-season Rest Between Sets
2 minutes

Pre-season Techniques
Pyramid — Increase the weight for each set while decreasing the number of reps you perform. This is the best technique for building muscle mass, developing strength, and explosive power.

Pre-season Aerobic Training
(Three times per week)
Workout 1 Jog 40 minutes
Workout 2 Run 20 minutes (hustle pace)
Workout 3 Sprints:
1 220 yd. full stride
2 100 yd. dashes
2 60 yd. dashes
2 40 yd. dashes
2 20 yd. dashes
2 10 yd. dashes

Pre-season Stretching
Full body stretch after all weight training and aerobic sessions. (See Chapter 26 for key body stretches.)

My Favorite
Training Programs for Golf

In-Season Training

Golfers play a lot of rounds, with golfing on weekends, during the week, and in tournaments. It's important to keep this in mind when continuing your training program throughout the season. I like to advise golfers to train twice a week with weights during the season. This seems to be enough to maintain the conditioning levels achieved in pre-season training, prevent injuries, and speed recovery if injuries do occur.

In-season Training Routine

Monday/Thursday — Whole Body
chest, back, shoulders, biceps, triceps, quadriceps, hamstrings, calves, lower back, abs

**Smith Machine
Bench Press**

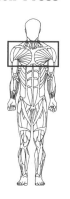

**Lat Pulldown
Wide Grip (be-
hind the neck)**

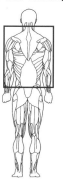

**Smith Machine
Shoulder Press
(front of the
neck)**

In-season

T
r
a
i
n
i
n
g

For
G
o
l
f

Barbell Arm Curl

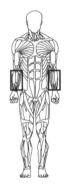

Barbell Wrist Curl

Bench Dip

In-season

Leg Press

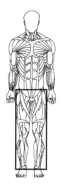  

Leg Extension

Leg Curl

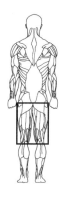  

In-season

Training for Golf

Smith Machine Standing Calf Raise

Broomstick Twists

Reverse Crunch

Hanging Leg Raises

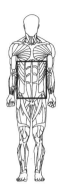

Hyperextension

Training for Golf

In-season

In-season Sets & Reps
Monday/Thursday — 2 sets of each exercise
1st set 10 reps, 2nd set 8 reps

In-season Poundages
All Upper Body Exercise
Increase weight 5-10 pounds per set

Lower Body Exercise — Leg Press, Squat, Calf Raise
Increase weight 10-20 pounds per set

Leg Extension and Leg Curl
Increase weight 5-10 pounds per set

Nonweight Assisted Exercise — Abdominals, Hyperextensions
Exercise to failure

In-season Rest Between Sets
1-2 minutes

In-season Techniques
Pyramid — Increase the weight for each set while decreasing the number of reps you perform. This is the best technique for building muscle mass, developing strength, and explosive power.

In-season Aerobic Training
None

In-season Stretching
Full body stretch after all weight training and aerobic sessions. (See Chapter 26 for key body stretches.)

Special Notes for In-season Training
Depending on match schedule, you may need to adjust weight training days. For example, if you have a match on Thursday night, move Thursday's weight training session to Friday.

For post-season golf training program see the All Sports Post Season Training Program section on page 353.

Training for Gymnastics

Pound per pound gymnasts have to be as strong as a power lifter. Hanging from bars and rings, and flipping on mats and balance beams requires incredible strength and balance. Gymnasts suffer a lot of injuries. Hurling the body through the air and crashing down on a mat can cause leg injuries. Likewise, swinging in circles while holding onto rings and catapulting through the air while clutching onto bars is equally damaging for the upper body.

My Favorite

Training Programs for the Gymnast

Pre-season Training

Pre-season gymnastics training is a very important training cycle for the athlete. Lifting weights and conditioning the cardiovascular system will prepare your body for the physical demands that the season will require. It is a time to focus on developing a good foundation of strength, endurance, flexibility, and explosive power.

This is best accomplished in the weight room by doing basic compound exercises such as bench presses, shoulder presses, and leg presses (exercises that put emphasis on the major muscle groups of the legs, chest and back). I also recommend special exercises for the forearms, incorporating specific exercises such as barbell wrist curls and exercises that work the pulling muscles — biceps and back muscles.

Pre-season Training Routine

Monday, Wednesday, Friday
Monday — Upper Body
chest, shoulders, triceps, abs

Wednesday — Lower Body
quadriceps, hamstrings, calves, lower back, abs

Friday — Upper Body
back, biceps, forearms, abs

Monday — Upper Body

Smith Machine Bench Press

Incline Dumbbell Press

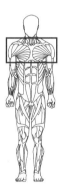

Smith Machine Shoulder Press (back of the neck)

245

Pre-season

Training For Gymnastics

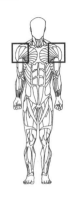

Dumbbell Lateral Raise

Bench Dips

Partial Incline Sit-up

Hanging Leg Raise

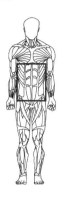

Leg Press

Wednesday — Lower Body

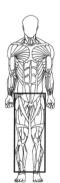

Smith Machine Squat

Pre-season

Training for Gymnastics

Dumbbell Step-ups

Leg Extension

Leg Curl

  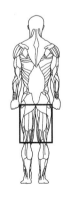

Pre-season

Smith Machine Standing Calf Raise

Seated Calf Machine

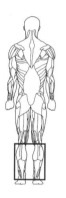

Crunch

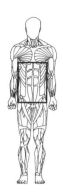

Training for Gymnastics

Pre-season

T r a i n i n g

For **G y m n a s t i c s**

Knee-ups Incline Bench

Hyperextension

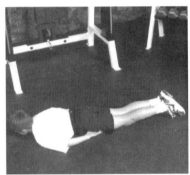  

Friday — Upper Body

Lat Pulldown Wide Grip (front of the neck)

Pre-season

Low Pulley Cable Row

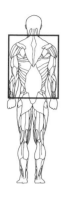

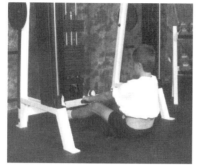 

Stiff Arm Pulldown

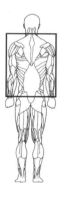

Two Arm Dumbbell Curl

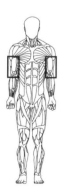

251

Pre-season

Train
For
Gymnastics

Reverse Barbell Curl

Barbell Wrist Curl

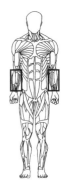

Pre-season

Pre-season Sets & Reps
Monday/Wednesday/Friday — 3 sets of each exercise
1st set 10 reps, 2nd set 8 reps, 3rd set 6 reps

Pre-season Poundages
All Upper Body Exercises
Increase weight 5-10 pounds per set

Lower Body Exercises — Leg Press, Squat, Calf Raise
Increase weight 10-20 pounds per set

Leg Extension and Leg Curl
Increase weight 5-10 pounds per set

Nonweight Assisted Exercises — Abdominals, Hyperextensions
Exercise to Failure

Pre-season Rest Between Sets
2 minutes

Pre-season Techniques
Pyramid — Increase the weight for each set while decreasing the number of reps you perform. This is the best technique for building muscle mass, developing strength, and explosive power.

Pre-season Aerobic Training (Three times per week)
Workout 1 Jog 40 minutes
Workout 2 Run 20 minutes (hustle pace)
Workout 3 Sprints:
1 220 yd. full stride
2 100 yd. dashes
2 60 yd. dashes
2 40 yd. dashes
2 20 yd. dashes
2 10 yd. dashes

Pre-season Stretching
Full body stretch after all weight training and aerobic sessions.
(See Chapter 26 for key body stretches.)

My Favorite

Training Programs for the Gymnast

In-Season Training

The name of the game for in-season training is to prevent injuries and maintain conditioning levels. Keeping your training program going throughout the season will help you maintain strength levels, prevent injuries, and help you finish the season strong and mentally fresh.

Let me caution you: In-season training is not the time to take risks in the weight room. In-season training involves training with weights at a minimum level — just enough to maintain conditioning levels.

In-season Training Routine

Monday/Thursday — Whole Body
chest, back, shoulders, biceps, triceps, quadriceps, hamstrings, calves, lower back, abs

**Smith Machine
Bench Press**

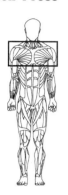

**Lat Pulldown
Wide Grip
(behind the neck)**

**Smith Machine
Shoulder Press
(front of the
neck)**

Training for Gymnastics

In-season

T
r
a
i
n
i
n
g

For

G
y
m
n
a
s
t
i
c
s

Barbell Arm Curl

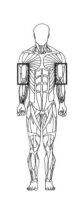

Barbell Wrist Curl

Bench Dips

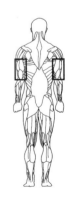

In-season

Angled Leg Press

Leg Extension

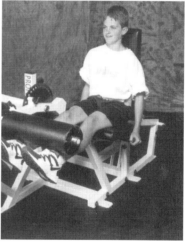

Leg Curl

Training for Gymnastics

257

In-season

Training for Gymnastics

For

Smith Machine Standing Calf Raise

Calf Raise on Leg Press

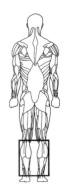

Crunch

In-season

Hanging Leg Raises

Hyperextension

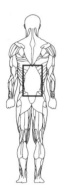

Training for Gymnastics

In-season

In-season Sets & Reps
Monday/Thursday — 2 sets of each exercise
1st set 10 reps, 2nd set 8 reps

In-season Poundages
All Upper Body Exercise
Increase weight 5-10 pounds per set

Lower Body Exercise — Leg Press, Squat, Calf Raise
Increase weight 10-20 pounds per set

Leg Extension and Leg Curl
Increase weight 5-10 pounds per set

Nonweight Assisted Exercise — Abdominals, Hyperextensions
Exercise to failure

In-season Rest Between Sets
1-2 minutes

In-season Techniques
Pyramid — Increase the weight for each set while decreasing the number of reps you perform. This is the best technique for building muscle mass, developing strength, and explosive power.

In-season Aerobic Training
None

In-season Stretching
Full body stretch after all weight training and aerobic sessions. (See Chapter 26 for key body stretches.)

Special Notes for In-season Training
Depending on meet schedule, you may need to adjust weight training days. For example, if you have a meet on Thursday night, move Thursday's weight training session to Friday.

For post-season gymnastics training program see the All Sports Post Season Training Program section on page 353.

Training for Soccer

19

Soccer is a sport that demands good cardiovascular conditioning, speed, agility, and good lower body strength and muscular endurance. In soccer, a player goes through many different movements, from jumping in the air, accelerating to kick a ball, jogging the length of a field, and changing direction quickly.

A good conditioning program will greatly enhance a player's ability to develop strength, power, and endurance, as well as to prevent and heal injuries.

My Favorite

Training Programs for Soccer

My Favorite Training Programs for Soccer

Pre-season soccer training is a very important training cycle for the athlete. Lifting weights and conditioning the cardiovascular system will prepare your body for the physical demands that the season will require. It is a time to focus on developing a good foundation of strength, endurance, flexibility, and explosive power.

This is best accomplished in the weight room by doing basic compound exercises such as bench presses, shoulder presses, and leg presses (exercises that put emphasis on the major muscle groups of the legs, chest, and back). I also recommend special attention for the legs, incorporating specific exercises such as step-ups and seated calf raises.

Pre-season Training Routine

Monday, Wednesday, Friday
Monday — Upper Body
chest, shoulders, triceps, abs

Wednesday — Lower Body
quadriceps, hamstrings, calves, lower back, abs

Friday — Upper Body
back, biceps, forearms, neck, abs

Monday — Upper Body

**Smith Machine
Bench Press**

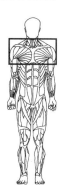

**Incline
Dumbbell Press**

**Smith Machine
Shoulder Press
(front of neck)**

Pre-season

Training For Soccer

Dumbbell Lateral Raise

Overhead Dumbbell Extension

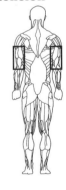

Partial Incline Sit-up

Pre-season

Hanging Leg Raise

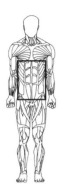

Leg Press

Wednesday — Lower Body

Smith Machine Squat

Pre-season

Training for Soccer

Dumbbell Step-Ups

Leg Extension

Leg Curl

Smith Machine Standing Calf Raise

Calf Raise on Leg Press Machine

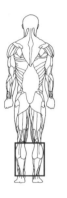

Crunch

Training for Soccer

Pre-season

T r a i n i n g

Knee-ups Incline Bench

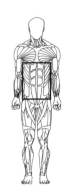

Hyperextension

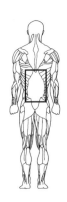

Friday — Upper Body

Lat Pulldown (front of the neck)

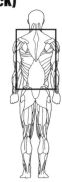

Pre-season

Low Pulley Cable Row

Stiff Arm Pulldown

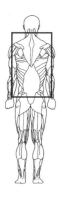  

Barbell Arm Curl

Training for Soccer

Pre-season

Training For Soccer

Low Pulley Arm Curl

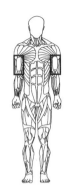

4-Way Neck Iso

Pre-season

Pre-season Sets & Reps
Monday/Wednesday/Friday — 3 sets of each exercise
1st set 10 reps, 2nd set 8 reps, 3rd set 6 reps

Pre-season Poundages
All Upper Body Exercises
Increase weight 5-10 pounds per set

Lower Body Exercises — Leg Press, Squat, Calf Raise
Increase weight 10-20 pounds per set

Leg Extension and Leg Curl
Increase weight 5-10 pounds per set

Nonweight Assisted Exercises — Neck Isos, Abdominals, Hyperextensions
Exercise to Failure

Pre-season Rest Between Sets
2 minutes

Pre-season Techniques
Pyramid — Increase the weight for each set while decreasing the number of reps you perform. This is the best technique for building muscle mass, developing strength, and explosive power.

Pre-season Aerobic Training (Three times per week)
Workout 1 Jog 40 minutes
Workout 2 Run 20 minutes (hustle pace)
Workout 3 Sprints:
1 220 yd. full stride
2 100 yd. dashes
2 60 yd. dashes
2 40 yd. dashes
2 20 yd. dashes
2 10 yd. dashes

Pre-season Stretching
Full body stretch after all weight training and aerobic sessions. (See Chapter 26 for key body stretches.)

My Favorite

Training Programs for Soccer

In-Season Training

Soccer players play a lot of games, with games on weekends, during the week, and tournaments. The season can get long and tiresome. It's important to keep this in mind when continuing your training program throughout the season. It's very easy with all the practice, games, and training to overtrain. I like to advise soccer players to train twice a week with weights during the season. This seems to be enough to maintain the conditioning levels achieved in pre-season training, prevent injuries, and speed recovery if injuries do occur.

In-season Training Routine

Monday/Thursday — Whole Body
Chest, back, shoulders, biceps, triceps, quadriceps, hamstrings, calves, lower back, neck, abs

**Smith Machine
Bench Press**

**Lat Pulldown
Wide Grip
(behind the neck)**

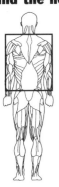

**Smith Machine
Shoulder Press
(front of the
neck)**

273

Training for Soccer

Barbell Arm Curl

**Overhead
Dumbbell
Extension**

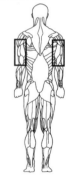

Leg Press

In-season

274

Leg Extension

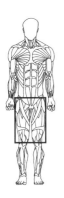
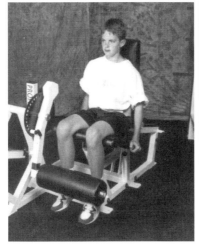
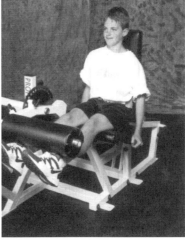

Leg Curl

Smith Machine Standing Calf Raise

In-season

T
r
a
i
n
i
n
g

For

S
o
c
c
e
r

Calf Raise (on Leg Press)

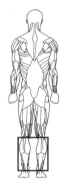

Crunch

Hanging Leg Raises

Hyperextension

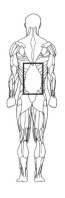  

4-Way Neck Iso

Training for Soccer

In-season

In-season Sets & Reps
Monday/Thursday — 2 sets of each exercise
1st set 10 reps, 2nd set 8 reps

In-season Poundages
All Upper Body Exercise
Increase weight 5-10 pounds per set

Lower Body Exercise — Leg Press, Squat, Calf Raise
Increase weight 10-20 pounds per set

Leg Extension and Leg Curl
Increase weight 5-10 pounds per set

Nonweight Assisted Exercise — Neck Iso, Abdominals, Hyperextensions
Exercise to failure

In-season Rest Between
Sets 1-2 minutes

In-season Techniques
Pyramid — Increase the weight for each set while decreasing the number of reps you perform. This is the best technique for building muscle mass, developing strength, and explosive power.

In-season Aerobic Training
None

In-season Stretching
Full body stretch after all weight training and aerobic sessions. (See Chapter 26 for key body stretches.)

Special Notes for In-season Training
Depending on game schedule, you may need to adjust weight training days. For example, if you have a game on Thursday night, move Thursday's weight training session to Friday.

For post-season soccer training program see the All Sports Post Season Training Program section on page 353.

Training for Wrestling

20

In high school, I was considered a small heavy weight. I can remember weighing in at the semi-state tournament at 205 pounds and feeling my heart drop as my four competitors weighed in at 245 pounds, 255 pounds, 285 pounds, and 300 pounds. During the entire season in my senior year, I only matched up two times pound per pound with my opponent. I gave up at least 20 to 30 pounds in almost every match. If I remember correctly, my senior year record was 22 wins and 8 losses. I obviously held my own and did remarkably well facing appointments who were much bigger than I. And there was one main reason for my success — a solid year-round training program. I was better conditioned and stronger, or at least as strong as many of my larger opponents.

I truly can attest to just how much a good year-round program can impact your performance as a wrestler. Other than learning the techniques, moves and intricacy of the sport, getting involved in a good training program will greatly elevate your performance.

Before I go further, I want to talk about something that concerns me in the sport of wrestling — cutting weight. I'm not a big fan of cutting with (losing weight to make a lower weight class.). Seldom, and I have been around a lot of wrestlers, have I seen anyone lose weight in a safe and effective manner. Losing weight is serious business that can cause serious long-term consequences to a person's health and well-being. I like to influence wrestlers to compete at the weight they are (given they are not 20 pounds off weight) and to develop themselves to get stronger, quicker, and more agile through a year round cycled training program. This is what I did to help me wrestle the opponents that were sometimes 70 to 80 pounds heavier than I was. I believe this is a much more intelligent and safer way to participate in the sport, and it doesn't result in any serious long-term health effects.

Because my views are not going to change the sport of wrestling and wrestlers will continue to "cut weight," at the end of Chapter 9 I include some guidelines as well as some "weight loss" danger signs. If you're cutting weight, you may wish to look them over. I the warning signs are there, then you may wish to rethink your weight loss strategy.

My Favorite
Training Programs for Wrestling

Pre-season Training

Pre-season wrestling training is a very important training cycle for the athlete. Lifting weights and conditioning the cardiovascular system will prepare your body for the physical demands that the season will require. It is a time to focus on developing a good foundation of strength, endurance, flexibility, and explosive power.

This is best accomplished in the weight room by doing basic compound exercises such as bench presses, squats, and power cleans (exercises that put emphasis on the major muscle groups of the legs, chest, and back). I also recommend special attention for the forearms, incorporating specific exercises such as barbell wrist curls and special exercises like step-ups to help further strengthen the legs.

Pre-season Training Routine

Monday, Wednesday, Friday
Monday — Upper Body
chest, shoulders, triceps, abs

Wednesday — Lower Body
quadriceps, hamstrings, calves, lower back, abs

Friday — Upper Body
back, biceps, forearms, neck, abs

281

Training

For **Wrestling**

Smith Machine Bench Press

Incline Dumbbell Press

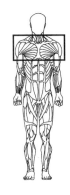

Smith Machine Shoulder Press

282

Dumbbell Lateral Raise

Dumbbell Front Raise

Bench Dips

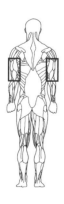

283

Training For Wrestling

For

Partial Incline Sit-up

Hanging Leg Raise

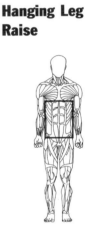

 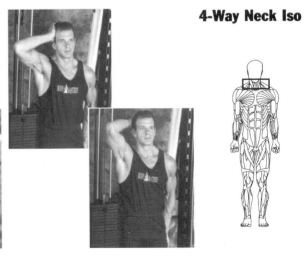

4-Way Neck Iso

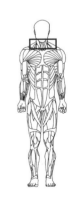

284

Wednesday — Lower Body

Barbell Power Clean

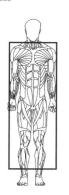

Leg Press

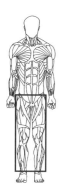

Smith Machine Squat

Pre-season

Training For Wrestling

Smith Machine Lunge

Leg Extension

Leg Curl

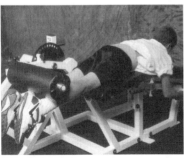 

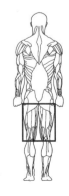

Pre-season

Smith Machine Standing Calf Raise

Calf Raise (on Leg Press)

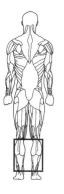

Crunch

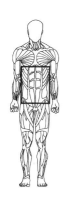

Pre-season

Knee-ups Incline Bench

  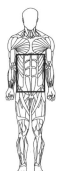

Hyperextension

  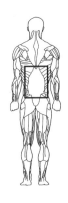

Friday — Upper Body

Lat Pulldown Wide Grip (behind the neck)

Pre-season

Low Pulley Cable Row

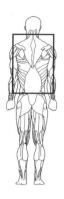

Dumbbell One Arm Row

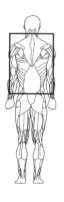

Barbell Arm Curl

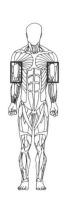

Training for Wrestling

Pre-season

T r a i n For **W r e s t l i n g**

Reverse Barbell Curl

Barbell Wrist Curls

 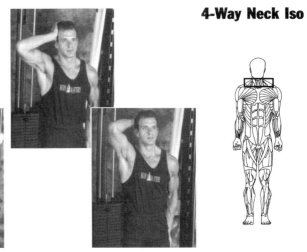

4-Way Neck Iso

Pre-season

Pre-season Sets & Reps
Monday/Wednesday/Friday — 3 sets of each exercise
1st set 10 reps, 2nd set 8 reps, 3rd set 6 reps

Pre-season Poundages
All Upper Body Exercises
Increase weight 5-10 pounds per set

Lower Body Exercises — Leg Press, Squat, Calf Raise
Increase weight 10-20 pounds per set

Leg Extension and Leg Curl
Increase weight 5-10 pounds per set

Nonweight Assisted Exercises — Neck Iso, Abdominals, Hyperextensions
Exercise to Failure

Pre-season Rest Between Sets
2 minutes

Pre-season Techniques
Pyramid — Increase the weight for each set while decreasing the number of reps you perform. This is the best technique for building muscle mass, developing strength, and explosive power.

Pre-season Aerobic Training (Three times per week)
Workout 1 Jog 40 minutes
Workout 2 Run 20 minutes (hustle pace)
Workout 3 Sprints:
1 220 yd. full stride
2 100 yd. dashes
2 60 yd. dashes
2 40 yd. dashes
2 20 yd. dashes
2 10 yd. dashes

Pre-season Stretching
Full body stretch after all weight training and aerobic sessions. (See Chapter 26 for key body stretches.)

My Favorite
Training Programs for Wrestling

In-Season Training

The wrestling season is long and physically demanding. Most wrestlers are exhausted and burned out by the time the tournaments roll around. Keeping your training program throughout the season will help maintain strength levels, prevent injuries, and help you finish the season strong and motivated to win.

In-season training is a maintenance program to maintain the condition levels built in the off-season. It is also a good way to prevent injuries and also to heal injuries that may occur during the season.

Let me caution you: In-season training is not the time to take risks in the weight room. In-season training involves training with weights at a minimum level — just enough to maintain conditioning levels.

In-season Training Routine

Monday/Thursday — Whole Body
chest, back, shoulders, biceps, triceps, quadriceps, hamstrings, calves, lower back, neck, abs

Smith Machine Bench Press

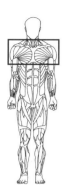

Lat Pulldown Wide Grip (behind the neck)

Smith Machine Shoulder Press (front of the neck)

Training For Wrestling

In-season

Training for Wrestling

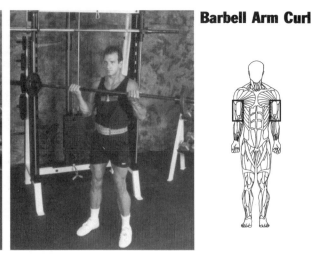

Barbell Arm Curl

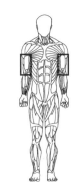

Tricep Cable Pushdown

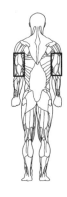

Leg Press

In-season

Leg Extension

Leg Curl

**Smith Machine
Standing Calf
Raise**

Training for Wrestling

In-season

T
r
a
i
n
i
n
g

For
W
r
e
s
t
l
i
n
g

Seated Calf Raise Machine

Crunch

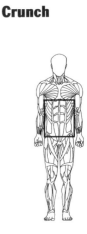

Hanging Leg Raises

In-season

Hyperextension

4-Way Neck Iso

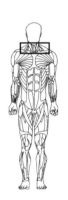

Training for Wrestling

In-season

In-season Sets & Reps
Monday/Thursday — 2 sets of each exercise
1st set 10 reps, 2nd set 8 reps

In-season Poundages
All Upper Body Exercise
Increase weight 5-10 pounds per set

Lower Body Exercise — Leg Press, Squat, Calf Raise
Increase weight 10-20 pounds per set

Leg Extension and Leg Curl
Increase weight 5-10 pounds per set

Nonweight Assisted Exercise — Neck Iso, Abdominals, Hyperextensions
Exercise to failure

In-season Rest Between Sets
1-2 minutes

In-season Techniques
Pyramid — Increase the weight for each set while decreasing the number of reps you perform. This is the best technique for building muscle mass, developing strength, and explosive power.

In-season Aerobic Training
None

In-season Stretching
Full body stretch after all weight training and aerobic sessions. (See Chapter 26 for key body stretches.)

For post-season wrestling training program see the All Sports Post Season Training Program section on page 353.

21 Training for Tennis

Tennis is a game that requires the foot speed of a boxer, the swinging power of a baseball player, the quickness of a sprinter, and the endurance of a long-distance runner. To be a good tennis player, you have to get into great shape.

Tennis players are susceptible to shoulder, lower back and forearm, and wrist injuries. I like to incorporate special exercises to strengthen these areas.

My Favorite

Training Programs for Tennis

Pre-season Training

Pre-season tennis training is a very important training cycle for the athlete. Lifting weights and conditioning the cardiovascular system will prepare your body for the physical demands that the season will require. It is a time to focus on developing a good foundation of size, strength, endurance, flexibility, and explosive power.

This is best accomplished in the weight room by doing basic compound exercises such as bench presses, squats, and power cleans (exercises that put emphasis on the major muscle groups of the legs, chest, and back). I also recommend special attention to the abdominals, wrists, forearms, and lower back.

Pre-season Training Routine

Monday, Wednesday, Friday
Monday — Upper Body
chest, shoulders, triceps, abs

Wednesday — Lower Body
quadriceps, hamstrings, calves, lower back, abs

Friday — Upper Body
back, biceps, forearms, abs

Monday — Upper Body

Smith Machine Bench Press

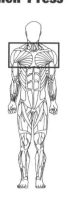

Incline Dumbbell Flys

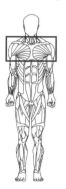

Smith Machine Shoulder Press

Training for Tennis

Pre-season

Training for Tennis

Dumbbell Lateral Raise

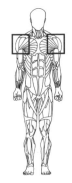

Tricep Cable Pushdown

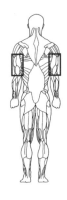

Broomstick Twists

Partial Incline Sit-up

Hanging Leg Raise

Leg Press

Wednesday — Lower Body

Pre-season

Training for Tennis

For

Dumbbell Squat

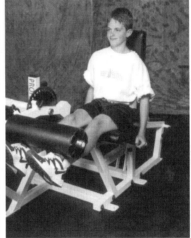

Leg Extension

Leg Curl

Pre-season

Smith Machine Standing Calf Raise

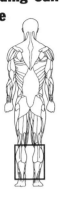

Calf Raise (on Leg Press)

Crunch

Training for Tennis

Pre-season

Training For Tennis

  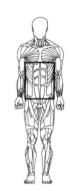

Knee-ups Incline Bench

   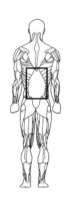

Hyperextension

Friday — Upper Body

Lat Pulldown Wide Grip (behind the neck)

Pre-season

306

Low Pulley Cable Row

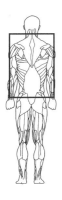

Two-Arm Dumbbell Curl

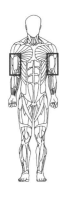

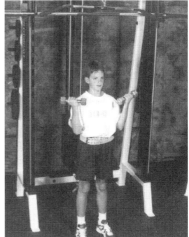

Hammer Dumbbell Curl

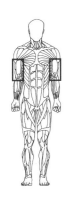

Pre-season

Training
For Tennis

Barbell Wrist Curls

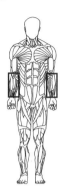

Pre-season Sets & Reps
Monday/Wednesday/Friday — 3 sets of each exercise
1st set 10 reps, 2nd set 8 reps, 3rd set 6 reps

Pre-season Poundages
All Upper Body Exercises
Increase weight 5-10 pounds per set

Lower Body Exercises — Leg Press, Squat, Calf Raise
Increase weight 10-20 pounds per set

Leg Extension and Leg Curl
Increase weight 5-10 pounds per set

Nonweight Assisted Exercises — Abdominals, Hyperextensions
Exercise to Failure

Pre-season Rest Between Sets
2 minutes

Pre-season Techniques
Pyramid — Increase the weight for each set while decreasing the number of reps you perform. This is the best technique for building muscle mass, developing strength, and explosive power.

Pre-season Aerobic Training (Three times per week)
Workout 1 Jog 40 minutes
Workout 2 Run 20 minutes (hustle pace)
Workout 3 Sprints:
1 220 yd. full stride
2 100 yd. dashes
2 60 yd. dashes
2 40 yd. dashes
2 20 yd. dashes
2 10 yd. dashes

Pre-season Stretching
Full body stretch after all weight training and aerobic sessions. (See Chapter 26 for key body stretches.)

Kris Gebhardt

My Favorite

Training Programs for Tennis

In-Season Training

Tennis players play a lot of matches, with games on weekends, during the week, and tournaments. The season can get long and tiresome. It's important to keep this in mind when continuing your training program throughout the season. I like to advise tennis players to train twice a week with weights during the season. This seems to be enough to maintain the conditioning levels achieved in pre-season training, prevent injuries, and speed recovery if injuries do occur.

In-season Training Routine

Monday/Thursday
Whole Body
chest, back, shoulders, biceps, triceps, forearms, quadriceps, hamstrings, calves, lower back, abs

**Smith Machine
Bench Press**

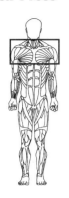

**Lat Pulldown
Wide Grip
(behind the neck)**

**Smith Machine
Shoulder Press
(front of the
neck)**

In-season

Training For Tennis

Two-Arm Dumbbell Curl

Barbell Wrist Curl

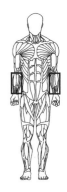

Tricep Cable Pushdown

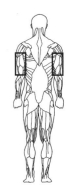

In-season

Leg Press

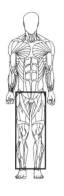

Leg Extension

Leg Curl

Training for Tennis

In-season

Training for Tennis

Smith Machine Standing Calf Raise

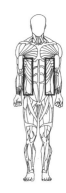

Broomstick Twists

Crunch

In-season

Hanging Leg Raises

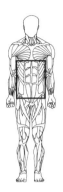

Hyperextension

In-season

In-season Sets & Reps
Monday/Thursday — 2 sets of each exercise
1st set 10 reps, 2nd set 8 reps

In-season Poundages
All Upper Body Exercise
Increase weight 5-10 pounds per set

Lower Body Exercise — Leg Press, Squat, Calf Raise
Increase weight 10-20 pounds per set

Leg Extension and Leg Curl
Increase weight 5-10 pounds per set

Nonweight Assisted Exercise — Neck Iso, Abdominals, Hyperextensions
Exercise to failure

In-season Rest Between Sets
1-2 minutes

In-season Techniques
Pyramid — Increase the weight for each set while decreasing the number of reps you perform. This is the best technique for building muscle mass, developing strength, and explosive power.

In-season Aerobic Training
None

In-season Stretching
Full body stretch after all weight training and aerobic sessions. (See Chapter 26 for key body stretches.)

Special Notes for In-season Training
Depending on your game schedule, you may need to adjust weight training days. For example, if you have a match on Thursday night, move Thursday's weight training session to Friday.

For post-season tennis training program see the All Sports Post Season Training Program section on page 353.

Training for Volleyball

22

Volleyball is a sport that demands good cardiovascular conditioning, speed, agility, good lower body strength, and muscular endurance. Volleyball players have to be able to move fast, change direction, jump high, and react in a split second.

Volleyball players need good leg strength to keep them jumping in the air, as well as good upper body strength to hit and spike the ball.

My Favorite
Training Programs for Volleyball

Pre-season Training

Pre-season volleyball training is a very important training cycle for the athlete. Lifting weights and conditioning the cardiovascular system will prepare your body for the physical demands that the season will require. It is a time to focus on developing a good foundation of strength, endurance, flexibility, and explosive power.

This is best accomplished in the weight room by doing basic compound exercises such as bench presses, shoulder presses, and leg presses (exercises that put emphasis on the major muscle groups of the legs, chest and back). I also recommend special attention to the legs, incorporating exercises such as step-ups, lunges, and some extra shoulder exercises like the front and side lateral raises.

Pre-season Training Routine

Monday, Wednesday, Friday
Monday — Upper Body
chest, shoulders, triceps, abs

Wednesday — Lower Body
quadriceps, hamstrings, calves, lower back, abs

Friday — Upper Body
back, biceps, forearms, abs

Monday — Upper Body

**Smith Machine
Bench Press**

**Incline
Dumbbell Press**

**Smith Machine
Shoulder Press
(Front of Neck)**

Training for Volleyball

Pre-season

T r a i n i n g

For

V o l l e y b a l l

Dumbbell Lateral Raise

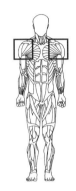

Dumbbell Front Raise

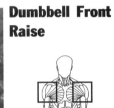

Bench Dips

Pre-season

Partial Incline Sit-up

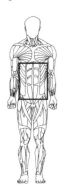

Hanging Leg Raise

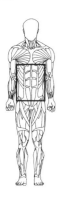

Leg Press

Wednesday — Lower Body

Training for Volleyball

Pre-season

Training for Volleyball

Smith Machine Squat

Smith Machine Lunge

 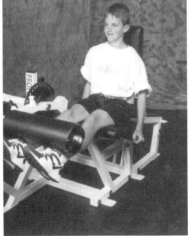

Leg Extension

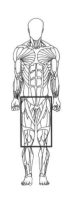

Pre-season

Leg Curl

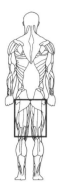

Smith Machine Standing Calf Raise

Calf Raise (Leg Press Machine)

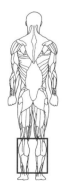

Pre-season

Training For Volleyball

Crunch

Knee-ups Incline Bench

Hyperextension

  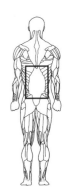

Pre-season

Lat Pulldown Wide Grip (be-hind the neck)

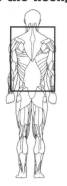

Low Pulley Cable Row

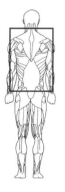

Stiff Arm Pulldown

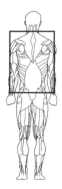

Training for Volleyball

Training For Volleyball

   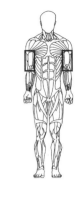

Two-Arm Dumbbell Curl

  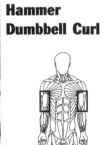

Hammer Dumbbell Curl

Barbell Wrist Curls

326

Pre-season

Pre-season Sets & Reps
Monday/Wednesday/Friday — 3 sets of each exercise
1st set 10 reps, 2nd set 8 reps, 3rd set 6 reps

Pre-season Poundages
All Upper Body Exercises
Increase weight 5-10 pounds per set

Lower Body Exercises — Leg Press, Squat, Calf Raise
Increase weight 10-20 pounds per set

Leg Extension and Leg Curl
Increase weight 5-10 pounds per set

Nonweight Assisted Exercises — Abdominals, Hyperextensions
Exercise to Failure

Pre-season Rest Between Sets
2 minutes

Pre-season Techniques
Pyramid — Increase the weight for each set while decreasing the number of reps you perform. This is the best technique for building muscle mass, developing strength, and explosive power.

Pre-season Aerobic Training (Three times per week)
Workout 1 Jog 40 minutes
Workout 2 Run 20 minutes (hustle pace)
Workout 3 Sprints:
1 220 yd. full stride
2 100 yd. dashes
2 60 yd. dashes
2 40 yd. dashes
2 20 yd. dashes
2 10 yd. dashes

Pre-season Stretching
Full body stretch after all weight training and aerobic sessions. (See Chapter 26 for key body stretches.)

My Favorite
Training Programs for Volleyball

In-Season Training

Volleyball players play a lot of matches, with games on weekends, during the week, and tournaments. The season can get long and tiresome. It's important to keep this in mind when continuing your training program throughout the season. I like to advise volleyball players to train twice a week with weights during the season. This seems to be enough to maintain the conditioning levels achieved in pre-season training, prevent injuries, and speed recovery if injuries do occur.

In-season Training Routine

Monday/Thursday
Whole Body
chest, back, shoulders, biceps, triceps, quadriceps, hamstrings, calves, lower back, abs

Smith Machine Bench Press

Lat Pulldown Wide Grip (behind the neck)

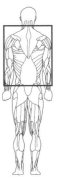

Smith Machine Shoulder Press (front of the neck)

In-season

Training For Volleyball

Two-Arm Dumbbell Curl

Barbell Wrist Curl

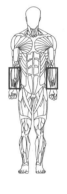

Overhead Dumbbell Extension

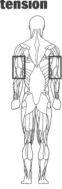

In-season

Angled Leg Press

Leg Extension

  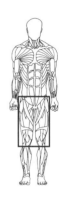

Leg Curl

  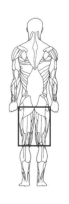

Training for Volleyball

In-season

Training For Volleyball

Smith Machine Standing Calf Raise

Calf Raise (on Leg Press Machine)

Crunches

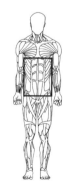

In-season

Hanging Leg Raises

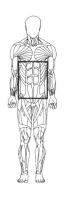

Hyperextension

 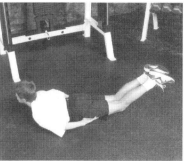

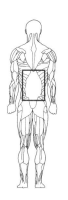

In-season

In-season Sets & Reps
Monday/Thursday — 2 sets of each exercise
1st set 10 reps, 2nd set 8 reps

In-season Poundages
All Upper Body Exercise
Increase weight 5-10 pounds per set

Lower Body Exercise — Leg Press, Squat, Calf Raise
Increase weight 10-20 pounds per set

Leg Extension and Leg Curl
Increase weight 5-10 pounds per set

Nonweight Assisted Exercise — Neck Iso, Abdominals, Hyperextensions
Exercise to failure

In-season Rest Between Sets
1-2 minutes

In-season Techniques
Pyramid — Increase the weight for each set while decreasing the number of reps you perform. This is the best technique for building muscle mass, developing strength, and explosive power.

In-season Aerobic Training
None

In-season Stretching
Full body stretch after all weight training and aerobic sessions. (See Chapter 26 for key body stretches.)

Special Notes for In-season Training
Depending on your game schedule, you may need to adjust weight training days. For example, if you have a match on Thursday night, move Thursday's weight training session to Friday.

For post-season volleyball training program see the All Sports Post Season Training Program section on page 353.

23 Training for Swimming

I want to dispel some myths about training with weights as a swimmer. Lifting weights properly will not cause you to become inflexible. As a matter of fact, lifting weights properly will increase your overall flexibility.

As a swimmer your goals are the same as any other athlete — to improve performance. Like in other sports, this is accomplished by becoming a better conditioned athlete.

Participating in a good year-round training program will help you increase strength, power, flexibility, and agility. You will also tone your muscles, increase muscular endurance, and give yourself the mental edge needed to be a peak performing athlete.

My Favorite

Training Programs for Swimming

Pre-season Training Program

Pre-season swimming training is a very important training cycle for the athlete. Lifting weights and conditioning the cardiovascular system will prepare your body for the physical demands that the season will require. It is a time to focus on developing a good foundation of strength, endurance, flexibility, and explosive power.

This is best accomplished in the weight room by doing basic compound exercises such as bench presses, shoulder presses, and leg presses (exercises that put emphasis on the major muscle groups of the legs, chest and back). I also recommend special attention for the legs, shoulders, abdominals, and lower back.

Pre-season Training Routine

Monday, Wednesday, Friday
Monday — Upper Body
chest, shoulders, triceps, abs

Wednesday — Lower Body
quadriceps, hamstrings, calves, lower back, abs

Friday — Upper Body
back, biceps, forearms, abs

Monday — Upper Body

**Smith Machine
Bench Press**

**Incline
Dumbbell Flys**

**Smith Machine
Shoulder Press
(back of the
neck)**

337

Pre-season

**T
r
a
i
n
i
n
g**

for

**S
w
i
m
m
i
m
g**

Pre-season

Dumbbell Lateral Raise

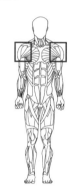

Bench Dips

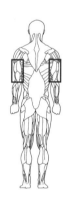

Partial Incline Sit-up

338

Incline Bench Knee-Ups

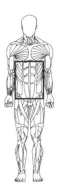

Leg Press

Wednesday — Lower Body

Smith Machine Squat

Training for Swimming

Pre-season

Training for Swimming

Smith Machine Lunge

 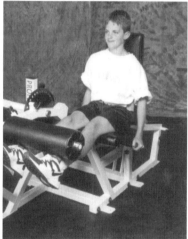

Leg Extension

Leg Curl

Pre-season

Smith Machine Standing Calf Raise

Seated Calf Machine

Crunches

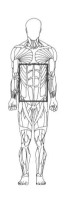

Training for Swimming

Pre-season

T
r
a
i
n
For
S
w
i
m
m
i
n
g

Pre-season

Leg Raise

  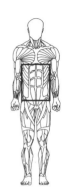

Hyperextension

  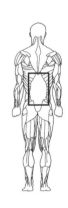

Friday — Upper Body

**Lat Pulldown
Wide Grip
(front of the
neck)**

Low Pulley Cable Row

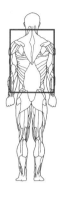

One-Arm Dumbbell Row

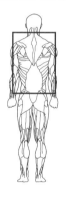

Two-Arm Dumbbell Curl

Training for Swimming

Pre-season

T r a i n i n g **S w i m m i n g**

Pre-season

Reverse Barbell Curl

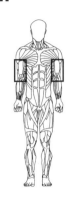

Cable Crunch

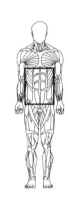

Broomstick Twists

Pre-season Sets & Reps
Monday/Wednesday/Friday — 3 sets of each exercise
1st set 10 reps, 2nd set 8 reps, 3rd set 6 reps

Pre-season Poundages
All Upper Body Exercises
Increase weight 5-10 pounds per set

Lower Body Exercises — Leg Press, Squat, Calf Raise
Increase weight 10-20 pounds per set

Leg Extension and Leg Curl
Increase weight 5-10 pounds per set

Nonweight Assisted Exercises — Abdominals, Hyperextensions
Exercise to Failure

Pre-season Rest Between Sets
2 minutes

Pre-season Techniques
Pyramid — Increase the weight for each set while decreasing the number of reps you perform. This is the best technique for building muscle mass, developing strength, and explosive power.

Pre-season Aerobic Training (Three times per week)
Workout 1 Jog 40 minutes
Workout 2 Run 20 minutes (hustle pace)
Workout 3 Sprints:
1 220 yd. full stride
2 100 yd. dashes
2 60 yd. dashes
2 40 yd. dashes
2 20 yd. dashes
2 10 yd. dashes

Pre-season Stretching
Full body stretch after all weight training and aerobic sessions. (See Chapter 26 for key body stretches.)

Kris Gebhardt

My Favorite
Training Programs for Swimming

In-Season Training

Swimmers have a lot of meets, and early morning practices. It's important to keep this in mind when continuing your training program throughout the season. It's very easy with all the practice, meets, and training to overtrain. I like to advise swimmers to train twice a week with weights during the season. This seems to be enough to maintain the conditioning levels achieved in pre-season training, prevent injuries, and speed recovery if injuries do occur.

In-season Training Routine

Monday/Thursday — Whole Body
chest, back, shoulders, biceps, triceps, quadriceps, hamstrings, calves, lower back, abs

**Smith Machine
Bench Press**

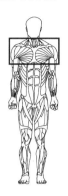

**Lat Pulldown
Wide Grip
(behind the neck)**

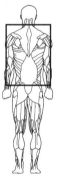

**Smith Machine
Shoulder Press
(front of the
neck)**

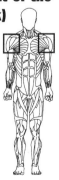

In-season

Training for Swimming

For

In-season

Two-Arm Dumbbell Curl

Tricep Cable Pushdown

Leg Press

348

Leg Extension

Leg Curl

Smith Machine Standing Calf Raise

Training for Swimming

In-season

Training

For

Swimming

In-season

Crunches

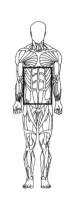

Hanging Leg Raises

Hyperextension

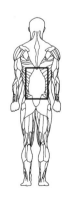

In-season Sets & Reps
Monday/Thursday — 2 sets of each exercise
1st set 10 reps, 2nd set 8 reps

In-season Poundages
All Upper Body Exercise
Increase weight 5-10 pounds per set

Lower Body Exercise — Leg Press, Squat, Calf Raise
Increase weight 10-20 pounds per set

Leg Extension and Leg Curl
Increase weight 5-10 pounds per set

Nonweight Assisted Exercise — Abdominals, Hyperextensions
Exercise to failure

In-season Rest Between Sets
1-2 minutes

In-season Techniques
Pyramid — Increase the weight for each set while decreasing the number of reps you perform. This is the best technique for building muscle mass, developing strength, and explosive power.

In-season Aerobic Training
None

In-season Stretching
Full body stretch after all weight training and aerobic sessions. (See Chapter 26 for key body stretches.)

Special Notes for In-season Training
Depending on your meet schedule, you may need to adjust weight training days. For example, if you have a game on Thursday night, move Thursday's weight training session to Friday.

For post-season swimming training program see the All Sports Post Season Training Program section on page 353.

All Sports

Post-Season
Training

Post-season training is a time to rehabilitate injuries, cycle down from hard training, get rest, and let the body recover. Quitting cold turkey in my opinion is not wise; it often leads to weight gain, deconditioning, depression, lethargy, and could extend the length of time it takes to recover from injuries. This approach — quitting "cold turkey" — usually leads to an athlete getting really out of shape. And this always makes it harder both mentally and physically to get the " engine " started again when the new season rolls around.

I do recommend some time off completely; however, I don't recommend that you abruptly stop and take long periods of time off from the weight room or from the running track.

The goals of post-season training are to: mend injuries, muscle aches and pains; maintain good body weight (muscle mass) and keep off bad body weight (fat); and, keep the mind sharp while maintaining a training regimen.

This can be accomplished very easily, without hours and hours spent in the weight and on the running track by implementing the post-season training program.

My Favorite
Post-Season Training Program

Post-season Training Routine

Monday/Thursday — Whole Body
Upper Body
chest, back, shoulders, biceps, triceps, neck, abs

Lower Body
quadriceps, hamstrings, calves, lower back, abs

Monday/Thursday

Chest Press Machine

Lat Pulldown Machine

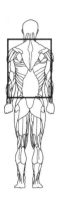

Shoulder Press Machine

Training

Post-season

Arm Curl Machine

Tricep Press Machine

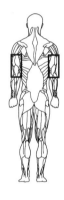

Leg Press Machine

Training

Post-season

Leg Extension Machine

Leg Curl Machine

Standing Calf Raise Machine

Training

Training

Abdominal Machine

Lower Back Machine

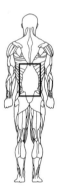

Post-season Sets & Reps
Monday — 2 sets of each exercise
1st set 10 reps, 2nd set 8 reps
Thursday — 2 sets of each exercise
1st set 12 reps, 2nd set 10 reps

Post-season Poundages
All Upper Body Exercises
Increase weight 5-10 pounds per set

Lower Body Exercises — Leg press, Squat, Calf Raise
Increase weight 10-20 pounds per set

Leg Extension and Leg Curl
Increase weight 5-10 pounds per set

Post-season Rest Between Sets
1-2 minutes

Post-season Techniques
Pyramid — Increase the weight for each set while at the same time decreasing the number of reps you perform. This is the best technique for building muscle mass as well as developing strength and explosive power.

Circuit — Here you perform a series of weight training exercises in a circuited manner, one after the other, with little rest in between reps and sets. Go from exercise to exercise, working each body part for one set, then repeating the circuit for the following set or sets.

Post-season Aerobic Training (two times per week)
Workout 1   40 minutes of jogging, treadmill, step climber, rowing machine, etc.
Workout 2   20 minutes (hustle pace) of running, treadmill, step climber, rowing machine, etc.

Post-season Stretching
Full body stretch after all weight training and aerobic sessions. (See Chapter 26 for key body stretches.)

Post-season Special Training Notes
Don't get yourself involved in long workouts. The circuit technique works really well for post-season training. You can get into the gym; then quickly

but effectively move through your training and go on and enjoy other activities. Remember this is a period of time off. The temptation will always be
there to add to the workout; however, this quickly turns into drudgery and
the workouts begin to get long and tiresome. Use this training period for
"active rest and recovery."

Training for Extreme Sports

MTV has done a lot to bring exposure to a new wave of radical sports called, Extreme Sports. They are adrenaline-pumping, fast-paced, high-risk activities that are not for the fainthearted. Some of the sports are so risky and dangerous that I won't waste my time on them. But many, such as snow boarding and stunt biking, can be fun and challenging activities.

Since many of the sports have a high risk for injuries, like flying through the air on a skateboard, crashing down on the handrail of the park steps, it's a great idea to be in excellent physical shape. Being in shape enables the body to better absorb falls, scrapes, bruises, twists, turns, and crashes, as well as to recover and heal itself. Also good strength, endurance, and muscle tone will make performing these sports a little easier.

My Favorite

Training Programs for Extreme Sports

Extreme Sports Training Routine

Monday/Thursday — Whole Body
chest, back, shoulders, biceps, triceps, abs, quadriceps, hamstrings, calves, lower back, abs

---

Monday/Thursday

**Smith Machine
Bench Press**

**Lat Pulldown
Wide Grip
(behind the
neck)**

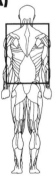

**Smith Machine
Shoulder Press
(front of the
neck)**

Training For Extreme Sports

Training For Extreme Sports

Barbell Arm Curl

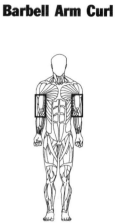

Tricep Cable Pushdown

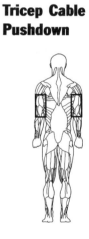

Leg Press

Smith Machine Squat

Leg Extension

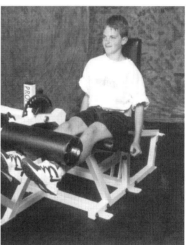

Leg Curl

Training for Extreme Sports

Training For Extreme Sports

Smith Machine Standing Calf Raise

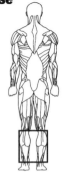

Crunch

Hanging Leg Raises

Hyperextension

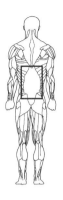  

Extreme Sports Sets & Reps
Monday/Thursday — 2 sets of each exercise
1st set 10 reps, 2nd set 8 reps

Extreme Sports Poundages
All Upper Body Exercises
Increase weight 5-10 pounds per set

Lower Body Exercises — Leg Press, Squat, Calf Raise
Increase weight 10-20 pounds per set

Leg Extension and Leg Curl
Increase weight 5-10 pounds per set

Nonweight Assisted Exercises — Abdominals, Hyperextensions
Exercise to Failure

Extreme Sports Rest Between Sets
1-2 minutes

Extreme Sports Techniques
Pyramid — Increase the weight for each set while decreasing the number of reps you perform. This is the best technique for building muscle mass, developing strength, and explosive power.

Extreme Sports Aerobic Training (Three times per week)
Workout 1 Jog 40 minutes
Workout 2 Run 20 minutes (hustle pace)
Workout 3 Sprints:
1 220 yd. full stride
2 100 yd. dashes
2 60 yd. dashes
2 40 yd. dashes
2 20 yd. dashes
2 10 yd. dashes

Extreme Sports Stretching
Full body stretch after all weight training and aerobic sessions. (See Chapter 26 for key body stretches.)

Training for
Speed Improvement

For many athletes, increasing speed is a goal for improving performance. There are few sports that speed does not play an important role. I can remember when I played football in college, we would do speed improvement drills and exercises in every practice. A quicker athlete is by far a better athlete.

Following the general fitness training program or any of the sports-specific training programs in this book will help you improve speed. A stronger, more powerful, flexible, in-shape person is able to run or move faster.

A few years ago, I stumbled onto something by accident that help me improve my sprinting speed so drastically that I could hardly get anyone to believe me — until they saw me run!

The last time I was officially tested in the 40-yard dash sprint was when I was in college. As a sophomore I ran the 40-yard dash in 5.4 seconds, which is not fast by any measure. I had never been much of a sprinter.

My brother is the head football coach for Kings High School in Kings Mills, Ohio. Every August, I make the trip over to watch his twice a day, pre-season football practices. On one of these trips, the team was doing conditioning drills, and my brother asked me if I would like to run 40-yard sprints with the team. I didn't want to make a fool of myself so I decided to run with the slower group — the offensive and defensive linemen. After running a couple of sprints, I realized that these guys were either slow as turtles or I had gotten faster because the sprints felt just like I was jogging. Surely, I thought, it's been twelve years and two knee surgeries since I ran sprints. I must just be running with a slow group.

One of the hot shot wide receivers shouted a challenge to me. He said, "Hey, why don't you run with us fast guys?" So I lined up with the fasted kid on the team for a show down. Hoping just to get barely beat, and not totally embarrassed, I was totally shocked when I crossed the 40-yard marker ahead of him. I thought, I got a good jump on him, so I raced him again, and a third time, winning all of the races. My speed was amazing.

After I went home that night, I was thinking about those races. I asked myself what I may have been doing that increased my speed so much. As I looked over my training, I realized that the big difference was that I was using a new leg training piece of equipment, called the Frank Zane Leg Blaster. At age 32, twelve years after any formal sprint training, coupled with two knee surgeries, I was running 40-yard dashes in the 4.7, 4.6 range!

My brother quickly summoned me to give him a clinic on the Frank Zane Leg Blaster. Speed improvement was one of his goals for his players, who were spending hours doing conventional drills and exercises, yet achieving only marginal results.

My Favorite
Speed Training Program

My speed training program requires the Frank Zane Leg Blaster. I have experimented and found that I did not get the same effect using a barbell. I believe this is because with a barbell, you have to worry about balancing the bar on your back when performing squats, lunges, and step-ups. With the leg blaster, the unique design of the weight carriage rests comfortably on your shoulder and distributes the weight evenly over your hips and thighs. With no undue pressure on your lower back you're able to perform exercises in a safe, more comfortable position. You're able to perform deep squatting exercises in a controlled self-spotting manner. This seems to develop the quadriceps more directly than the traditional barbell that causes you to tilt forward and inhibits your ability to descend deep into the squat movement.

This is the leg workout that I was doing that helped me improve my speed so dramatically. I was training my legs once a week doing the following exercises in this order:

- ◆ Leg Blaster Squat   4 sets of between 8-15 reps*
- ◆ Leg Blaster Step-ups   2 sets of between 10-15 reps*
- ◆ Leg Blaster Lunge   2 sets of between 8-12 reps*
- ◆ Leg Blaster Sissy Squat   1 set of between 15-20 reps*
- ◆ Leg Blaster Calf Raise   2 sets of between 15-20 reps*
- ◆ Hanging Leg Raises   3 sets of between 15-25 reps*

*Increase weight 5-10 pounds per set

Training For Speed Improvement

Leg Blaster Squat

Leg Blaster Step-ups

Leg Blaster Lunge

Leg Blaster Sissy Squat

Leg Blaster Calf Raise

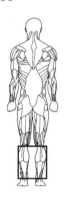

Hanging Leg Raises

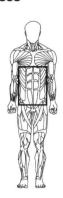

Training for Speed Improvement

Generally there are three things that will help you increase your speed — increase your flexibility, increase your strength, and develop the technical skills of running. Using the leg blaster, I was able to increase my leg strength, increase my range of motion, and flexibility.

Give this workout a try, I highly recommend that you talk your coach into buying a commercial leg blaster for your school weight room, or that you by the home or commercial model to use at home. For more information on the Frank Zane Leg Blaster, call 1-800-643-2412.

26
Training for Stretching & Flexibility

One of the easiest ways to improve performance in sports, relieve tightness and tension, as well as add shape to the body in a general fitness program can be accomplished with little exertion and effort through stretching.

Stretching exercises are without a doubt the easiest exercises to execute in any training program. They're easy to do, require little effort, and you don't need equipment or fancy facilities. And they even can be done at any level of skill.

Stretching can be defined as the act of extending beyond the current limits. Stretching results in flexibility. Flexibility can be defined, for our purposes, as the range of motion of a joint or limb. Stretching the muscles of the body allows the joints to become more pliable. Then the limb moves more freely, and the range of motion increases.

Stretching is not only good for improving the range of motion of the joints, but stretching has many other benefits including:

- Improves strength through the range of motion
- Prevents muscle soreness and injuries
- Helps shape and define muscles
- Relieves tension

Stretching and Training

Stretching and training go hand-in-hand. In every sport, flexibility greatly improves the athletes ability to perform. Tight, rigid, inflexible muscles and joints cause athletes to perform sluggishly, inhibit technique, and dulls the skills, which often results in aches, soreness, pain, and injuries. One of the best ways to run faster and jump higher and is by stretching. Stretching is also an important ingredient of developing strong, powerful, shapely, defined and well-toned muscles.

Stretching before training helps prepare the joints and muscles for motion and helps avoid needless injuries. Stretching during training, helps keep the target area warm and limber, and it also creates awareness or that "pump feel" in the muscle or muscles being trained. Stretching after training is a great way to cool down from training and prevent muscle soreness.

My Rules for Safe and Effective Stretching

- Stretch before, during, and after training
- Never bounce, jerk, or bob...ease slowly into each stretch
- Hold each stretch for 15-30 seconds
- Always stretch the entire body during every training session
- Avoid stretches that cause pain beyond temporary discomfort
- Increase the range of motion in each new training session
- Stretch extra tight areas twice

My Favorite
Full Body Stretches

The following eleven full body stretches have become my favorites over the years. Keep in mind, there are many stretching exercises. However, I have discovered that these work really well my clients and me. Give them a try, and if you like them, add them to your program.

Neck Stretch (Repeat opposite side)

Doorway Chest Stretch

Two-Arm Pull Lat Stretch

Training for Flexibility

T r a i n i n g

For

F l e x i b i l i t y

Hand-Over-Hand Mid/Upper Back Stretch (Repeat Opposite Side)

Face Down/Arms Up Shoulder Stretch

One-Arm Over-head/Tricep Stretch (Repeat Opposite Side)

Two-Arm Back/ Bicep Stretch

Leg Kickover/ Lower Back and Hip Stretch

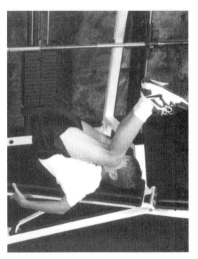

Leg Forward Hamstring Stretch (Repeat Opposite Side)

Training for Flexibility

Training For Flexibility

One-Leg Up/ Quadricep Stretch (Repeat Opposite Side)

Foot-on/Step Calf Stretch (Repeat Opposite Side)

Conclusion

You will only get out of stretching what you put into it. Take it seriously. Apply the guidelines that I gave you: Always stretch before, during, and after training, and you will enjoy the many benefits of good flexibility.

Injuries & Overtraining

Training seriously for twenty years, as well as participating in twelve years of competitive sports, you can bet I have had my share of injuries. I've had two knee surgeries in one year, bouts with a nasty sciatica, a severely pinched nerve in my right shoulder, and about fourteen bouts of pinched nerves in my lower back.

In all likelihood, if you're training hard, participating in sports, there is a good chance the you will suffer from an injury at some time or another.

Most injuries are not devastating. With proper rest, combined with good rehabilitation and nutrition, you will mend in no time at all.

Training Injuries
There are many types of injuries you might encounter in training and sports. There are injuries to muscles, bones, tendons, and ligaments which usually occur as strains, sprains, dislocations, fractures, and breaks.

The obvious serious injuries like breaks,

fractures, dislocations, and severe strains and sprains require immediate medical attention. That's the only solution. Do not ever attempt to self-remedy a serious injury.

For the most part, most training injuries are muscle related and are not severe enough to warrant medical attention. These injuries often occur for several reasons:

- Improper or no warm-up
- Lack of flexibility
- Reaching beyond current conditioning/overstraining
- Overloading an unhealed injury
- Underdeveloped muscle or muscles
- Carelessness
- Poor technique or skill execution
- Overtraining

Most muscle injuries can be self-treated. Ice and heat treatments, light training or light rehabilitation exercises, and rest, along with good supplementation will have you back to training or in the game in no time.

If you're lucky, your school has a good athletic training program, and you can get diagnosis and treatment from the team trainer. If not, there are simple treatments to administer such as light icing and heat that will speed the healing of injuries and which will help relieve the temporary discomfort.

Remember for severe injuries like tendon and ligament injuries, play it safe and see a doctor.

For Your Mental Attitude

Injuries not only put a strain on you physically, but they can be mentally painful or stressful as well. Many athletes report that during injuries they experience:

- Depression
- Loss of motivation
- Frustration
- Anxiety
- Loss of appetite

Injuries are a part of high intensity training and sports. The mental outlook you have on injuries will make the difference in your ability to deal with the setbacks and the time off for rehabilitation. I know that it's disappointing to be going along, making really good progress, and then to have it halted because of a nagging injury. Or maybe you've worked so hard in the off-season, only to get hurt during the first week of practice.

But injuries don't have to be a time of gloom and despair. Time off for injuries can be a positive and productive time. With the right attitude, you can use the time wisely to improve the other aspects of your training or game.

You can:

- ◆ Develop the mental side of the game
- ◆ Use the time to train the rest of your body
- ◆ Work on becoming more aerobically fit
- ◆ Reevaluate your training program
- ◆ Overhaul your diet

Some injuries are so severe that they can put an end to your career. I personally have experienced this. One morning in my junior year in college, I sat in a doctor's office and listened to him tell me to give up playing football. My knee was in such bad shape that it was going to require surgery. I was having so much pain and discomfort that I could barely walk. That day, right in that office, after ten years of sweating, training, and practice, my football career ended.

What You Can Do to Avoid Injuries
Prevention is the best medicine. This can be done in many ways. Conditioning — getting in good shape and staying there. Keeping personal stress levels down. Get plenty of rest. I always recommend at least eight hours of sleep for hard training athletes. Learn to perform, relaxed and in control. This is accomplished through hours and hours of practice. Eat a healthy diet and take supplements. Always warm up and stretch prior to training or practice.

Overtraining
You would think that if a little training is good then a lot of training would be better. It seems logical. Getting one "A" on a report card is good, but getting four is better. Putting more points on the scoreboard is better insurance that you're going to win.

But in training, it's a little different. Sometimes more is not better. Sometimes more is actually less.

Exercise, sports, and training all break the body down. In weight training for instance, when you curl a dumbbell, you actually damage the muscle fibers of the arm. As a matter of fact, they don't grow, or get stronger, until they have rested and rebuilt themselves. The results come after the training, in the rest phase.

Training the body too hard or too often does not allow it to recover and forces it into a state called overtraining. It's a damaging state which creates muscle loss, drains energy, and lowers the immune system.

Probably the biggest culprit of injuries in training and sports is overtraining. This can occur for many reasons: doing too much too soon; not getting enough rest; a poor diet; and a poorly designed training program.

To be a peak performing athlete, it's important that you learn the signs of overtraining and how to combat it if it happens to you. In all likelihood, if you're training hard, participating in more than one sport, you will experience it at some time. It's important that you heed the warning signs of overtraining so you can take the appropriate actions to rectify it.

Common Signs of Overtraining

- Loss of appetite
- Irritability
- Lack of motivation
- Excessive muscle soreness, aches, and pains
- Nagging injury
- Loss of body weight
- Illness — colds, flu, etc.
- Decrease in performance
- Significant loss of strength

When overtraining occurs, it's best to immediately take measures to counter it. Usually by making immediate changes in your training, practice schedule, diet, and rest patterns, you can eliminate the symptoms quickly and easily.

How to Combat Overtraining

- Change your training routine
- Get extra rest
- Take a day off from training
- Cut your training time down
- Take extra supplements
- Increase your quality food intake

Conclusion

- Injuries are a part of being physically active. Some injuries are serious and can require immediate medical attention. Others are not so serious and can be treated using ice, heat, and rest.
- Overtraining is when you train too hard and too often. The warning signs indicate that immediate changes need to be made to your routine, diet, and rest schedule.
- Remember the best medicine for injuries is prevention. If an injury occurs, get immediate treatment. Learn to recognize the signs of overtraining and you will have a long athletic career.

28 The Importance of Supplements

Dietary supplements are the safest, most effective way to insure that your body is getting all the vital nutrients it needs to perform at its best. Today, there are a variety of supplements on the market available in nutrition stores, health food stores, mail order, etc.

Recently my son started taking supplements. A couple of times a day he blends together skim milk, ice cubes, a banana, and a scoop of High Performance Optimizer Metabolic Optimizing powder, and a teaspoon of natural peanut butter. After just about three weeks on the supplements, he lost body fat, increased muscle mass, got stronger, and was able to shave a minute off his best two-mile time in cross county. He feels like his energy has increased quite a bit. He also has noticed a change in his eating. He no longer craves as many sweets.

Are Supplements "Miracle Workers?"
Though manufacturers would like for you to believe so, supplements are not

miracle or wonder products. They are merely concentrated food sources -- protein, carbohydrates, fats, minerals, and vitamins. Nutritional supplementation can be very complicated and confusing. I am constantly sorting through all the hype and testing new products.

And the debate over the real benefits of supplementation continues. The pro-supplement group is typically made up of athletes and top trainers who claim that there are benefits to supplementing your diet. The anti-supplement group is typically made up of people who are not athletes, including some doctors, nutritionists, and dieticians who say that if you eat right, you won't need to supplement your diet. Round and round they go creating confusion.

When I use supplements, I feel better. My body is leaner. I'm stronger and I recover from my training sessions more quickly. Therefore, I continue to use them and recommend them to all my clients.

Supplements are important because they:

- ♦ Ensure that your body gets an adequate supply of nutrients which are essential for energy, growth, repair, and recovery
- ♦ Help your body to recover more quickly from hard training
- ♦ Help to control cravings and wean you from undesirable foods

Choosing Supplements

Today's supplements are far improved over the ones that were available when I was a teenager. The products now available mix easily, taste like a really good milkshake, and are widely available in nutrition stores and through mail order companies. Supplement manufacturers offer a wide variety of flavors, packaging, and mixing options as well. They products have also advanced way beyond simple protein powders.

Yet with all the manufacturers stating that their products are the best and with new products coming out almost daily, choosing supplements can be very confusing.

When choosing supplements, individual consider-ations should be taken into account, such as per-sonal characteristics, body type, individual needs, and training goals. Choosing supplements wisely in most cases means getting help from the experts, but not everyone can give expert advice. I have found that if you stick with the products manufactured by the top companies, you really can't go wrong.

My favorite companies are:

♦ Optimum
♦ TwinLab
♦ Champion
♦ Weider
♦ Met-rx
♦ Universal

All make good products that are high in nutrients, low in sugars and hidden fats.

Before you go into a store, get your goals in mind and read the product labels. Most are self-explanatory. And by all means ask for advice from the people who work in the stores; it's their business to know the products that they sell.

Note: Stay away from products that promise results that seem too good to be true, such as lose 10 pounds in a week or put on 20 pounds of muscle in a three days. These are tricks to get you to buy low quality products (in most cases).

Guidelines for Using Supplements

Everyone, especially teenagers, should use supplements in addition to eat-ing regular meals. I do not recommend that teenagers use supplements as meal replacements. My son Kraig still eats three meals a day, even though he uses supplements. The supplements are used for between meal and be-fore bedtime nutritious snacks.

Supplements that offer good combination of nutrients -- vitamins, minerals, complex carbohydrates, proteins, fats, and special ingredients for growth, repair, and recovery, are the way to go. These products are available in powder form in a wide variety of flavors. They also offer users many options for mixing, baking, and drinking.

I also like many of the nutrition bars that are currently on the market. I have found through my own use that these work well as in-between meal snacks and are tasty little desserts for after meals. And they're very handy to take along when you're on the go.

Again, the rule of thumb is to stick with products from the top manufacturers.

My Favorite Way to Take Supplements

Buying vitamins, minerals, proteins, and recovery ingredients separately is very confusing and can be extremely time consuming. Scientists and manufacturers have done us a big favor by developing all inclusive supplements. They've taken the guesswork out of the complicated science of nutritional supplementation.

All inclusive formulas such as Optimum Nutrition's Anabolic Activator III powder combines and blends all the vitamins, minerals, proteins, fats, carbohydrates, and special recovery ingredients into an easy to blend shake mix.

Give my shake recipe by mixing in a blender the following ingredients:

> 6-8 medium ice cubes
> 6-8 ounces of skim milk
> 1-2 scoops of supplement powder (see label for recommended serving)
> 1 banana
> Blend for 60 seconds.

Viola — the easiest, best-tasting way to take supplements.

Don't Break the Bank

If you have been in a nutrition store or sporting goods store that sells supplements, you were probably shocked at many of the prices. Some of these supplements are really expensive.

There is no reason to break the bank. Many of the really good supplements are not the most expensive. Optimum Nutrition's High Performance Optimizer powder comes in a 3.2 pound container and will last the average teenager a couple of months. It sells for $23.95, which is very reasonable when you figure the cost per serving. And it's a lot cheaper than a bag of chips.

Conclusion

- ◆ For growing teenagers, who want to be healthy, control weight, safely lose weight, gain weight, exercise, and eat right, supplements are a must.
- ◆ For teenagers involved in sports, training, and intensive exercise, supplements are again a must.
- ◆ Insuring that the body is getting all the nutrients it needs to grow, perform, repair itself, and recover from the stresses of sports, exercise, activity, and every day living, supplements are an excellent insurance policy for the body.

29 Training At Home

Rarely will you see anyone get an "A" in a class without having done some homework. Likewise, rarely will you get into great shape or reach the peak of athletic performance without doing a fair share of training homework.

Training at home can be a great way for those who are not involved in sports, as well as a great place for those involve in sports to get in additional training. It's also a great place for athletes to train pre-season and post-season, especially if the school doesn't have the staff or resources to train athletes year round.

When I was in high school, I did my fair share of training at home. I'm convinced that being able to walk on and earn a scholarship in college was a direct result of the many hours I trained at home. Today, all my training (except when I'm traveling) is done in my basement using my home gym equipment.

When I was involved in direct sales, I sold millions of dollars of home exercise equipment to people who set up home gyms in their houses, apartments, and condos. Home gyms can be a great place to train as long as you follow certain guidelines.

Benefits of a Home Gym

There are many benefits and advantages to having a home gym. Home gyms are practical. They:

- ◆ Save you time
- ◆ Are easily accessible
- ◆ Are convenient
- ◆ Allow you to have access to good equipment
- ◆ Never close
- ◆ You don't have to rush through your training
- ◆ Plus there's no peer pressure

What is a Home Gym?

A home gym is any area in the home equipped with anything from a few dumbbells to enough equipment to fill a small health club. My home gym rivals any health club and is stocked with better equipment than most. However, my first home gym consisted of a pair of dumbbells and a bench. Though rudimentary in design and sparsely equipped, my first home gym gave me excellent results, good enough to go onto college and earn a scholarship.

Home Gym Equipment

When I talk about fitness equipment, I am referring to two specific kinds of equipment -- cardiovascular equipment like treadmill, exercise bikes, and rowing machines, and weight training equipment like minigyms, barbells, and dumbbells.

Cardiovascular Training Equipment

Any piece of exercise equipment with a primary function of training the cardiovascular system (heart, lungs, respiratory system) is considered cardiovascular exercise equipment. The most popular pieces of cardiovascular equipment for the home gym are the treadmill, step climbers, stationary bike, ski machine, and rowing machine.

The Treadmill

The electric treadmill is an excellent choice for the

home gym. The versatility of the treadmill allows you to cross train. You can use it a variety of ways to alleviate boredom and obtain enhanced results. Using the treadmill requires that you include your whole body in the workout. The arms have to coordinate with the lower body in order to keep the pace, thus allowing you to exercise from head to toe.

Step Climber
Another good choice for the home gym. The step climber is designed to simulate step climbing and offers an excellent aerobic workout and tones the legs as well.

Stationary Bikes
The stationary bike has been around for years and was probably the first piece of exercise equipment made for the home gym. Today, you can find top quality stationary bikes in basically three categories: the traditional upright, the traditional upright with upper body action, and the newer recumbent-style bikes.

The upright stationary bike is great for low impact aerobic exercise. It's gently on the body, while offering the user leg toning, heart rate elevation, and calorie burning.

The stationary bike with upper body action made famous by Schwinn (the AirDyne) gave the user something to do with his/her upper body while pedaling away. The added movement allows you to:

♦ Increase the intensity of your workout
♦ Increase your heart rate, and
♦ Burn more calories

The recumbent exercise bike with its bucket seat design allows you to sit comfortably while you pedal your legs in front of you in a more horizontal position. The concept in this innovative design is comfort with the added bonus of better blood flow because the heart and legs are on the same plain. You also get a better workout for the lower abdominals, glutes, and hamstrings.

Ski Machines
Providing a good aerobic workout, the ski machine simulated the sport of cross-country skiing. For the most part, Nordic Track deserves all of the credit for the popularity of the ski machine. Cross-country skiing is a strenuous activity, requiring stamina, coordination, and an abundance of motivation.

Rowing Machines
Rowing offers a very good aerobic workout. It helps to tone and strengthen the abdominals, back, biceps, hips, thighs, hamstrings, and calves.

Resistance Training Equipment
Also referred to as weight training equipment, resistance training equipment is designed to strengthen, build, tone, and develop muscle mass. You'll find this equipment in three basic categories: weight machines, free weights, and free weight equipment (benches, racks, etc.).

Weight Machines
Here, resistance is developed via a weight stack. Using a selector pin, you choose the desired weight and perform the exercise. Of the many kinds of weight machines available for the home gym, you'll find primarily two configurations -- minigyms weight machines and single station weight machines.

Minigyms
Minigyms combine several weight lifting movements into one machine and are probably the most popular additions to the home gym. The minigym is a sensible, economical machine to purchase because, for example, you can perform the chest press, shoulder press, lat pulldown, and leg extension/leg curl all on one machine.

Minigyms can be classified by the number of weight stacks. For example, we refer to a minigym that has a single stack of weights for performing all of the exercises as a one-stack minigym. A minigym with four weight stacks is a four-stack machine. The advantage of having more weight stacks is that more than one person can use the machine at the same time, and the exercises work better because no action is compromised by the limits of having only one stack. The main exercises a minigym should offer are: chest press, pec-butterfly, shoulder press, lat pulldown, low pulley, leg extension, leg curl, and leg press.

Single Station Weight Machines

Single station weight machines, sometimes referred to as selectorized weight machines (the machines you find most often in health clubs, corporate fitness centers, institutions, etc.) are becoming more prevalent in home gyms. The single station weight machine is designed to perform primarily one exercise and operate using its own weight stack.

Since the machine is made to perform only one exercise, all of the design emphasis has been centered around one function. You won't find any compromises on any part of the machine; therefore, the end result is a more biomechanically correct machine — a more functional machine that allows you to isolate and work a target muscle or muscle group more precisely and effectively.

There are single station machines available for just about every weight-lifting movement. It can take as many as eight to twenty machines to make up a complete circuit. The most common single weight machines are:

- Seated Chest Press
- Pec-Deck Fly
- Lat Pulldown
- Seated Row
- Shoulder Press
- Lateral Deltoid Raise
- Bicep Arm Curl
- Tricep Extension
- Abdominal Crunch
- Lower Back
- Leg Press
- Leg Extension
- Lying Leg Curl
- Calf Raise

Free Weights

The oldest, most recognizable and probably the best form of weight training equipment are free weights — barbells and dumbbells. They are inexpensive, will last forever, require no maintenance, take up very little floor space, and are ideal for a home gym. Barbells consist of a bar, four to seven feet long, weight plates varying in poundage from 2 1/2 pounds to 45 pounds, and collars to keep the weight plates from slipping off the bar. There are two kinds of barbells — Olympic and Standard.

Olympic barbells, the more popular of the two, have two-inch holes in the plates and two-inch drums or cylinders on the ends of the bar.

Standard barbells have one inch holes in the plates and bars, one inch in diameter.

Note: The Olympic barbells have heavier bars (around 45 pounds); therefore, the lowest amount of weight you will lift using an Olympic set is 45 pounds. The standard bar weights only 10-15 pounds.

Dumbbells
These are miniature barbells designed to be held individually in each hand. Dumbbells are the most versatile piece of weight training equipment. They offer the user the freedom to perform many weight lifting movements that machines and barbells don't. There are many styles of dumbbells available:

- ◆ Hexagonal — solid cast, hexagonal-shape dumbbell
- ◆ Round Head — solid cast with a round end
- ◆ Pro-style — made with standard weight plates permanently welded or locked onto the bar

Adjustable dumbbells — available in either standard one-inch hole or the two-inch Olympic style, made so that you can change the weight by adding or removing the weight plates.

Free Weight Equipment
Although you can use barbells and dumbbells alone, many exercises require that you use a bench or rack. For example, in order to perform the dumbbell chest press or dumbbell flys, you must use a flat bench. Without this bench, you cannot perform these exercises.

Free Weight Benches
Weight benches are affordable and offer many weight training options.

Olympic Bench
An Olympic bench is a flat bench that has upright weight holders space about 44 inches apart. The advantage of this bench is that it holds the bar and weight directly at the point of lockout on the chest press exercise, allowing the user to begin and end the exercise safely because the user racks and unracks the weight at the user's strongest position (arms locked out). Olympic-style benches accommodate seven-foot Olympic and standard bars.

Standard Bench

This bench is identical to the Olympic bench except that the uprights are spaced closer together. If you like wide grips and want to use bars shorter than seven feet long, the standard bench is your choice.

Utility Benches

Utility benches offer many exercise options for dumbbells, barbells, and even weightless exercises which make the utility bench a must for the home gym. The most common utility benches available are:

Flat Bench — used in a reclined, horizontal position. The dumbbell chest press, dumbbell flys, and the seat arm curls are just a few of the many exercises that can be performed on this bench.

Incline Bench — used in a tilted 20-60 degree angle. Dumbbell incline flys, dumbbell incline presses, etc. can be performed on this bench.

Decline Bench — used in a tilted declined 20-45 degree position; this is perfect for sit-ups, decline dumbbell flys, decline dumbbell presses, etc.

Combination Flat and Incline — two benches in one, combining the flat bench and incline bench.

Combination Flat, Incline, and *Decline Bench* — a combination of three benches; the adjustability of this bench allows the user to perform a multitude of exercises.

Free Weight Systems

Combination benches are designed to allow the user to perform many basic exercises. The combination bench includes attachments that allow the user to perform many exercises that are performed on a minigym. The more common combination benches adjust for bench presses, incline presses, and shoulder presses. Their attachments allow the user to perform leg extension and leg curls, lat pulldowns, low rows, preacher arm curls, pec butterflies, and squats.

Smith Machines

The Smith Machine is the most popular and versatile piece of weight training equipment for the home gym. It's my favorite.

The Smith Machine is designed to allow the user to perform free weight exercises, such as bench presses, squats, shoulder presses, etc. in complete safety. The machine is composed of a barbell attached to vertical guide rods via linear bearings. As you lift the weight, the bar travels up and down the vertical guide rods. You can stop or bail out any point during the lift by rotating the bar. When your rotate the bar, giant hooks lock into any of the many safety pegs along the plane of travel.

The main advantage of the Smith Machine is that, as you lift, the guide rods keep the bar in a constant vertical plane of travel, allowing you to simulate many traditional free weight movements without danger of losing control. Advantages to using the Smith Machine:

- Teaches correct form
- Safety
- Extremely effective for squats
- Great for doing pressing movements — especially behind the neck presses

Power Stations
There are many versions of the power station that will allow you to perform many free weight movements. Most equipment manufacturers offer some version of a power workout station which usually consists of a rack, an adjustable bench, and a leg extension and leg curl attachment. Many manufacturers make Smith Machines and free weight systems.

Which is Better — Free Weights or Machines?
This debate will go on forever.

Weight machines offer safety and ease of use by guiding and supporting the lifter through the range of motion. They offer variety, reduce boredom, provide for isolated movements, and make some exercises more comfortable to perform.

Free weights are extremely versatile, providing an unlimited variety of angles and movement. Free weights help to develop coordination and balance, and are relatively inexpensive. They require little floor space and are somewhat portable.

Both free weights and weight machines are important for developing a balanced physique. I suggest that you incorporate both in your training program, if possible. For instance, you might train at school with barbells and dumbbells, and train at home with a minigym.

The Best Place to Purchase Training Equipment?
There are many places that sell good-quality fitness equipment. Stores that

specialize in selling only fitness equipment are your best bet, since they usually carry only the best brands.

Conclusion

Whatever kind of home gym you choose, remember home can be a great place to train. Follow the same rules that you follow in a school. A gym is a serious place — don't participate in horseplay, avoid distractions, put your weights back, keep the room clean, and avoid clutter. Try always to train with a partner or have someone close by in case you need a spotter.

The right equipment offers the tools you need to accomplish some great goals — getting into fantastic shape and supercharging your sports performance.

Remember these important points when setting up your home gym:

- Establish your training goals.
- Evaluate equipment options.
- Designate a comfortable place in your home where you will enjoy training.
- Get expert instruction on how to use the equipment properly.

For detailed information on equipment models and manufacturers, see my book, *Body Mastery*, which is available in many bookstores or by calling 1-800-643-2412.

30

Drug-free Training

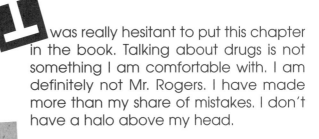

I was really hesitant to put this chapter in the book. Talking about drugs is not something I am comfortable with. I am definitely not Mr. Rogers. I have made more than my share of mistakes. I don't have a halo above my head.

Yet, my publisher has repeatedly encouraged me to include this chapter, because of my experience with twenty years of drug-free training. I have never used any performance-enhancing drugs, something that is quite rare for someone who has spent more than half his life in the gym.

The sport of bodybuilding has turned into a pharmaceutical nightmare. Drugs are everywhere. If you pick up a recent issue of your favorite magazine, the advertisements will blow your mind. There are page after page of advertisements promoting diuretics, growth hormones, steroids — drugs you can't even pronounce.

Having worked for a sheriff's department

just outside the suburbs of Detroit, you can imagine what I was exposed to on a daily basis. I saw people destroying their lives. I'm not talking about street bums. I processed doctors, lawyers, and housewives through the county jail daily — all throwing their lives away on a drug habit. Of course, the drugs they were taking were other types, not performance-enhancing drugs. But their stories were similar; they were dependent on the drug to perform — just not in the gym.

I was shocked when I stepped into the fitness business and learned how much drug use there was in a "health" promoting business. So it's impossible to write about training, especially weight training without addressing the issue of drugs. This won't be a sermon. I'm only going to share with you what I learned over the years, just as I did in the other chapters of this book.

What I Learned about Performance-enhancing Drugs

When I was a sophomore in college a group of about seven or eight guys decided to really impress the coaches during winter workouts by going on steroids. If you impress the coaches during winter workouts, then you get moved to the front of the depth chart for spring practices. In other words, you earn a starting position — the goal of every player! Winter workouts are very important.

This group of guys would get their weekly shots and show up for workouts. Almost overnight their bodies were transforming. They were making progress double, triple, even quadruple of what the rest of us were making. I was beginning to get worried. As a walk on, I had to constantly prove myself or I did not get any money. I was fighting for my scholarship. If I didn't get any money, then I could not stay in school.

The coaches were sky high on these seven players. Routinely they would point out their achievements and make statements like, "We wish everyone would work as hard these guys." As each week passed, my friends and I were getting more and more worried. We were beginning to look like we were loafers because our results seemed minuscule to the others. An increase of ten pounds looked like nothing to the drug-assisted 30, 40, and even 50 pound increases.

One of the big strength contests during the winter was the leg press contest. It consisted of leg pressing as much weight as possible one time. The goal was 1,000 pounds. Nobody on this team had led pressed 1,000 pounds, so it was becoming quite a contest. During every workout someone would give a gallant try but fall short.

I had not even entered the contest, figuring I could not compete with the guys who were on the "juice." These guys were all closing in around 900 pounds. It was very clear that one of them was going to hit the 1,000 pound mark really soon.

After my training session one day, several of us (who were not doing drugs) were sitting around feeling down, complaining about how it was unfair that the guys on the "juice" were getting favorable attention from the coaches. We felt like quitting. One of my friends suggested that maybe we should all get on the "juice," — after all we came here to play, not to sit on the bench.

I told my friends that it wouldn't be worth it. When I started training at 14, my first coach Ron Weiglib said, "You'll make better progress over the long haul by not taking drugs." He likened it to the fable of the tortoise and the hare. I explained to them that the other guys were only experiencing temporary gains, and these gains would disappear as soon as they got off the drugs. And although our gains seemed rather insignificant, our progress would be permanent.

My friends all looked at me like I was nuts. They were seeing phenomenal increases in the seven or eight players using drugs.

During the next team workout, the leg press contest was on. Two of the guys who were using drugs were dueling for the crown. Both attempted 900 and failed. It looked like the record had been eluded again.

For some strange reason that day, I stepped up to the leg press and said load it to 1,000. You should have seen the look in the eyes of everyone around. The coaches had a "get real" look in their eyes. Many of the players began to laugh. I know what they were thinking: "What is this sophomore doing thinking he can compete with the big guys?"

As I strapped in the leg press, I counted each of the 45 pound plats to make sure that it was indeed 1,000 pounds. The carriage of the leg press could not hold another plate. It was so full of 45 pound that you could not even get a 2 1/2 pound plate on it if you wanted to. The entire gym went silent as I prepared to make the attempt. Right as I was getting ready to start, I thought, "This is a time to show those guys on the juice that slow and steady wins the race. Small, continual, real gains are what matter in the end." I kept thinking, "I have been lifting for five years. I have worked slowly to make steady progress. I am real. My results are real. I will do this lift."

As the carriage unlatched and the 1000 pounds of weight released onto my legs, the crowd stepped back. With every ounce of might, I watched the plates coming down, getting closer and closer. When the leg press came to a halt, I exploded with the force of a rocket and the 1,000 pounds began to move to the top of the leg press machine. Although it seemed like a half hour, in seconds it was all over. The record had been set; 1,000 pounds went up that day by a "natural."

You should have seen the faces when I got up and walked away. Jaws hit the ground.

I was extremely proud that day, not because of the record lift, but because of the lesson it affirmed. You don't need drugs to be a winner. Soon after I made the 1,000 pound attempt, six other guys made the same record. Four of the six were drug-free.

After winter workouts, spring football began. The guys who were on the drugs had to get off them because of the threats of testing by the league. Many got injured. Others suffered physically, losing weight and strength daily. Their performances declined. My performance only got better. I finished the spring strong, without injury, and in a good enough position to earn my scholarship. What a lesson we all learned that year!

Threats of Health Risks
People who play to win often take challenges, take chances, and risks. Making drugs illegal is not going to make the difference, neither is reminding them of the health risks.

It was not the threat of physical harm or the legal consequences of drug use that caused me to stay away from them. I was never that concerned with the health risks or the threat of jail. I was concerned with the psychological risks involved with using drugs.

Anytime you gain success or results by using something outside of yourself, you begin to rely on it and come to believe that you can't perform without it. Soon it becomes an addiction. You've got to have it. It begins to control your success.

When you succeed based on what you have achieved and strived for, the results are "real." You know you produced them, not some drug. You never have to rely on something else to make you succeed. As it relates to training, you gain a much clearer picture of your progress, because you know what's working and what is not. If you're taking a drug and you succeed, you don't know if it was the drug, your diet, or your training.

Going at It Naturally

According to an article in the April 1994 issue of *Muscle and Fitness Magazine*, it's estimated that 90 percent of male professional bodybuilders and 80 percent of female bodybuilders use steroids.

Someone who trains naturally can't expect to get the results reported in many books and magazine written by or for professional bodybuilders. Of course, I'm not suggesting that all bodybuilders use drugs.

But herein lies the problem. Many of us pick up these magazines, and see a photograph of an attractive professional bodybuilder, and turn to read the article on how they built a beautiful body in ten weeks. Then we adopt their training program, drive ourselves to achieve what the article promises, and end up overtrained, frustrated with our lack of results, or perhaps even injured.

We don't fail to reach the promised goals because we didn't try hard enough. We failed because we haven't been given all of the information.

The needs of the natural athlete are different than the needs of a drug-assisted athlete. My training philosophy is centered around a natural training program. It gives you all the information you'll need to achieve your goals unassisted by drugs. Just remember, it's important not to judge those who choose the drug-assisted approach. That's their choice, and their right.

But be aware that drug-free training will test your patience and your character. You are going to have to work hard while watching those who are using drugs progress more quickly with less effort. Keep in mind that your success will be true success. With commitment, you will eventually win out over those who take the other path.

I picked up my first dumbbell when I was 14, and it wasn't long after that that I was exposed to the pharmaceutical side of training. Fortunately I had a very good teacher and coach who taught me to shy way from the quick fix approach. He taught me the real meaning of training from the start, training for individual development — to improve your natural abilities.

Only You Can Decide

As an athlete in today's world, you will be exposed to drugs. I was, you will, and so will your kids and your kids' kids. Drugs will never be wiped out. People will always try to look for the answers outside of themselves.

As a young adult you will have make the decision — an important decision.

Remember, these are my views, and they may be different from yours, your friends, coaches, and parents. But that's okay. Ultimately it is up to you to decide whether to take the drug-free training approach or the drug-assisted route. In life, there will be many forks in the road. This is one of them.

Whatever choice you make, or have made, remember you made it. No one else is responsible for your actions. You are responsible for the outcome. If you have made a bad one, learn from it and move on. It's never too late to change.

Remember, training naturally without the use of drugs requires intelligence and patience. Slow and steady wins the race.

P a r t

Total Mind Training

The first two-thirds of this book was spent on training the body. I would have preferred to make the first part of the book this section, "Total Mind Training," because your mind is the leader of the body.

When I speak of your mind I am not referring to tissue, cells, or actual brain lobe. I am referring to your intellect, your thought processes.

The next eleven chapters are devoted to getting your mind into shape. They are designed with mental exercises that will strengthen, tone, and condition your "intellect" By strengthening and building your mind, you will become a more physically fit person, a better athlete, and improve your skills — all around.

In my studies of elite athletes, successful business people, peak performers as well as my own experience, I have found that the common factor in all great achievers is how they use their minds — even more than their bodies. Looking back over my training career, I have noticed that with each succeeding year I get more mentally involved in my training, and I do less physical work. But, I keep getting into better and better shape every year.

Train your brain like you train your body

The following chapters are filled with "intellectual" exercises. Use them to build a strong mind. A strong mind equals a strong body. With my favorite brain-building exercises, you will learn how to:

- Develop a winners mind-set
- Mentally prepare for training
- Talk to yourself
- Become a peak performer
- Change your attitude to affect your performances
- Set goals
- Develop mental toughness
- Find mentors and models
- See yourself succeed

In all experiences that I have had with people, I have come to the conclusion that two things are for sure:

- We become what we think about.
- You have to train your mind to be a winner, a success, a peak performer.

Conclusion

Use the mental exercises and "intellectual nutrition" in the following chapters to build your mind, learn how to become a winner, develop your mental toughness, and nurture good relationships.

Each exercise is designed to challenge you intellectually and build your mind power. There are varying degrees of difficulty, just as there are with weight training. You need to increase the reps and the amount of weight you lift to keep developing physically. So it is with these exercises, which if practiced regularly, will help you become a peak performer. Each will challenge you in different ways, some will be easier than others.

Ask any world class athlete what separates them from the others and they will say it's not necessarily what they do physically; after all everyone lifts weights, everyone practices the same moves. It's what they do mentally that makes them a winner.

Remember that these exercises not only apply to sports; you can use these new skills throughout your life, as you enter the working word, and in personal relationships.

31
Creating a
Winner's Mind-set

osing is no fun. And while winning is definitely not everything, it is extremely important in life. Some day you will go for a job interview, and you can rest assured you will not be the only candidate. In order to get the job you must win out over all the others. It's that simple. Life is full of contests. If you win in the interview, you get the job; if you lose, you don't.

If you are going to participate in sports, go out some day and compete in the job market, or start and run a successful business, then you are going to have become a winner!

Winners Aren't Born, They Are Made

Very few people realize that the ability to win is not a birthright. In other words people who succeed were not born to be winners. They win because they have taught themselves how to become winners. They have trained and developed themselves, with hours of study, practice, and participation. Becoming a winner is a skill you can learn, but you must be willing to work at it.

Everyone thinks Michael Jordon was born a basketball star. But did you know that he was cut from his high school team? Did you know he had to get up early every morning to practice before school just to make the team? Michael Jordon taught himself how to be a winner.

A lot of people argue that success depends upon genetics, heredity,talent, luck... Could others really be born more gifted than we are? It may be possible, but it's hard to believe that every professional athlete was born with the talents and the skills needed to make the team. When I look at the rosters of the NFL teams, I often see players who were too slow and too small to play professional football. And the same is true when I look at the Olympic athletes, I see stories of triumph — athletes who had to overcome enormous obstacles and challenges.

It's crystal clear to me that winners are made not born! It's always easy to make excuses why success belongs to the other person. But winners really take the responsibility and put in the work it takes.

Over the years I have studied hundreds and hundreds of winners from all walks of life — athletes and business leaders. After studying their lives, their actions, and their accomplishments, I have come to the conclusion that there are eight keys to becoming a winner.

1. Create a Winning Environment
In my research of winners, there is one thing that stands out. They create winning environments. They surround themselves with other winners. The people closest to them, that influence them on a daily basis, are are chosen carefully. Winners know that people are like chameleons; they blend into their environment.

One of the first things you need to do in order to become a winner is to take a look around you. Who are the people in your life? What are they doing with their own lives? Are they pursuing positive goals, like working towards a degree and saving money to go to college?

Make sure that you are careful with whom you associate. Choose friends and situations wisely. Work to always surround yourself with the right people: people who support your best interests and goals.

2. Establish Value for Yourself
Winners have high value for themselves. They respect their minds and bodies. They take stock in their unique talents and gifts.They seldom take foolish challenges, or take unnecessary chances with their life or safety. They al-

ways place importance on themselves and weigh actions against consequences. And they always work to increase their personal value.

Work at establishing a value for yourself. Continually increase your value by participating in activities that build your character. Realize your uniqueness; you are not replaceable. There will never be another you. The mold has been broken.

3. Develop Your Mental Toughness

Winners work diligently at developing their mental toughness. They realize the more mentally tough they become, the better they will be able to handle challenges, obstacles, and fears. As you will learn in Chapter 40, developing mental toughness takes work It's quite involved, but well worth the investment of time and energy.

4. Set Goals

This is a quote I will always remember: "A ship that sets sail without a destination never arrives." This is so true. A person without goals never goes anywhere or achieves anything.

Winners set goals. They decide what they want and then set up a plan to get it. They map it, chart the course they are going to take, and then lock their minds onto it.

Do you know where you want to go? Do you have a plan? Work at writing down your goals. Set up a list of things you want to accomplish. Study Chapter 38 on goal setting. Learn the mechanics of setting and achieving goals.

5. Work on Developing a Winner's Personality

The winners I studied all seemed to have similar personality traits. They all had high qualities of appreciation and gratitude, excitement, passion, determination, persistence, and confidence.

Winners appreciate and are grateful for the the opportunity to develop and express their talents. They show appreciation openly to those who help them, like parents, coaches, friends, and teammates. They are thankful for the opportunity to be able to participate in the activities of their choosing, that highlight their talents and interests. And they realize that many people have worked to make it possible for them to partake and succeed.

Winners are excited about what they are doing. They practice and play with enthusiasm. They face challenges with a positive attitude, realizing that the "why" they do something is sometimes more important than "how" they do it.

Winners are passionate about their training and performance. They get emotionally involved. They realize that you cannot put forth much effort if your heart is not in it.

Winners are determined people. They set their minds on their tasks and go to work on their goals. They cannot be easily persuaded off their course. They have drive to help them get through obstacles and road blocks. They have an unwavering determination to succeed with their goals.

Confidence is a critical trait of winner. They realize that with confidence they can relax and to let themselves perform their best. They build their confidence by mastering skills.

Work at developing these personality traits:

- ♦ Learn to appreciate others.
- ♦ Get excited about your goals.
- ♦ Be passionate — put your heart into everything you do.
- ♦ Be determined — become like a guided missle to hit your targets.
- ♦ Develop your confidence.

6. Work Harder
Winners are hard workers. They are always willing to put in the effort. They know the key ingredient to success is sweat. Being a winner is not about being in the right place at the right time, or luck of the draw. Working hard is the payment for all achievement and winners know this. They are willing to pay the price. This may mean studying while your friends are out partying, working to save for college, or putting overtime in the gym.

7. Be a Leader
Winners are leaders. They take responsibility and are willing to step out in front. Winners lead by example; they set the tone with their actions. Their walk becomes their talk.

Be willing to accept the challenge that leadership offers.

8. Set Up a Success Library
One of the things that I am ashamed to admit to you is that I was 20 years old when I finally read my first book cover to cover. Since that day I have read hundreds of books, on subjects such as self-help, physical training, nutrition, business, finances, and personal relationships.

Winners know that reading something of substance, something of value, and something that increases knowledge makes them grow — on and off the field. They know that reading is feeding the mind.

Set up a success library. Read books and magazines on personal development. Study the biographies of great athletes and successful business people.

Success always leaves clues.

Conclusion

There are very few limitations on what you can accomplish. Self-doubt and a lack of winner's traits are surefire ways to become a loser. A positive mental attitude can literally move mountains, put astronauts in space, win gold metals, and build a successful business. Spend time cultivating these eight winners traits.

Just as you train your body with weights to get stronger, spend time training your mind. And always remember: "Winners aren't born; they are made."

Make yourself a winner!

32 Mentally Preparing for Training & Sports

Anyone who has ever competed would agree with the this statement: The toughest opponent one faces is the "inner critic" deep inside of each of us. This is the person inside our minds that talks to us nonstop.

Sometimes this "inner voice" is helpful, giving us positive feedback, like, "You're doing a great job," or "C'mon, push it. You're a winner." Sometimes this inner voice is negative, and says, "You are so slow," or, "You can't do it. It's too tough."

High achievers, winners, and champions have shown us that what we say to ourselves makes the difference between winning and losing. The winners are able to use their inner voices to "talk" themselves into victory and succeeding. A losing effort is many times a reflection of negative, pessimistic, and gloomy thoughts. These thoughts are self-defeating.

It's important to know that performance is always a reflection of inner thoughts. What we say to ourselves makes a difference in how we perform before, during, and after training, practice, and the game.

We all need this critic, especially athletes. The critic serves as a coach, pointing out weakness that we need to strengthen. Understanding the positive side of constructive criticism makes it easier to accept and use in a positive way. Inner criticism such as, "You were not as fast as the guy who beat you," should be used to structure a more productive off-season training program.

Three Important Ways to Use Your Inner Voice

Become aware of what you say to yourself. Examine how it impacts your performance as well as your life. Pay attention to what you were thinking before, during, and after training, practice, and competition.

Learn to use your inner voice in a positive way. As you become more aware of what you say to yourself, you will realize the impact of your thoughts on your performance. You will begin to see the connection between positive, productive thoughts and success, as well as negative, unconstructive thoughts that lead to bad performance.

Replace negative criticisms with positive feedback. Unfortunately many of us hurt our potential, by focusing on the negative. We all make mistakes. And instead of using the experience in a positive way, to make changes to improve our behavior, we waste time and energy feeling guilty and stupid about our weaknesses. Using positive thoughts and words as a replacement for negative criticisms, we can reprogram ourselves with new beliefs that enhance our performance.

Performing in the Zone

Peak performance involves a course of physical and psychological processes working together . Peak performance requires the ability to transcend deep into the activity. Concentration and focus — freedom from distraction — are qualities that you need to develop in order for you to get the most out of your performances.

This is often referred to as getting into the performance "zone." Great athletes often speak of this while recalling peak performances. The zone could be defined as a centered state with extraordinary clarity and focus. You become connected — that is — become one with your actions.

This state is not achieved by simply going through the motions. Complete focus and attention is must. Peak performance is not something achieved by showing up. Nor is it achieved by rushing through your training in order to get it over with.

I have a pre "zone" performance checklist that I use before training. Give it a try.

- ◆ Do I know my skill?
- ◆ Have I rested?
- ◆ Am I relaxed?
- ◆ Am I free from distractions with focused awareness?
- ◆ Does my body have the right nutrients?
- ◆ I am focused on the present moment?
- ◆ Am I using mistakes as a teacher and learn from them?
- ◆ Am I concentrating only on the things that I can control?
- ◆ Am I honest with myself, catching myself anytime I become negative and immediately turn it positive?
- ◆ Am I confident in my abilities?
- ◆ Are my objectives clear?
- ◆ Have I visually rehearsed my performance?
- ◆ Am I prepared?
- ◆ Am I in controlled over my intensity?

Practice Makes Perfect

Many people complain about practice and training. They moan about how much effort it takes and how many hours they have to spend doing it.

Practice is a necessary skill you will have to learn to enjoy if you are every going to become proficient at anything in your life.

There are two ways to view practice and training:

- ◆ Negatively — It's work or drudgery.
- ◆ Positively — I am improving my skills. I am becoming a better athlete and person.

Practice is a time for connecting not reflecting. If you spend time comparing yourself to others, their skill level and abilities, you will never enjoy a day of practice. Practice is a time for you to sharpen your individual skills. In a team sport, it's a time for players to sharpen their individual skills and talents, then unite with teammates to choreograph their joint talents and skills.

Great performances are achieved through the accumulation of successful training and practice sessions — many of them. Continually remind yourself of this. Make this a part of your growing awareness as a winner.

Conclusion

The process of mentally preparing for training and sports begins when you recognize, use, and take control of your "inner voice."

- Think of this inner voice as a coach. Use the feedback as a guide to make adjustments in your efforts. Welcome it.
- Training free from distractions, with clarity and focus comes from honing your performance skills.
- Practice is part of the equation of peak performance. All great performances are the result of hours and hours of preparation. View practice as positive activity. See the big picture. Practice is an investment in your overall self-development.

What to Say When You Talk to Yourself

By talking to yourself, you can program your mind for success. Recent scientific discoveries have shown that what you think and say actually cause physical and biochemical changes in your body.

Have you ever really thought about what you say to yourself? You have hundreds of mini-conversations with yourself daily. Are you having constructive conversations, mentally patting yourself on the back when you need to? Or, are you constantly telling yourself things like: "Why am I so dumb, so slow, so clumsy, so fat?"

How many times have you said something like, "I don't have the talent?" Have you ever analyzed each of the words you direct toward yourself? How many of these things wouldn't you say to your best friend or even to your worst enemy?

Self-Talk
Through carefully guided self-talk

— positive conversations you carry on with yourself — you can consciously program your subconscious mind by feeding it with constructive words and phrases aimed at helping you to reach your goals. Self-talk is a psychologically sound method of programing the subconscious mind to affect your behavior.

Speaking the Right Language

We communicate our thoughts and beliefs through external dialogue (communication with others) and through internal dialogue (communication with ourselves). Words are the messengers of our thoughts, and our thoughts create who and what we become.

How do you talk about yourself? Do you say good or bad things about yourself?

Become conscious of all of the words and phrases you use to talk about yourself. Carefully analyze each and every word. Learn to pay particular attention to how you describe yourself to others. Watch out for phrases, such as, "I can't . . . ," "I'll never have . . . ," "I am not talented enough."

Eliminate these negative words and phrases from your vocabulary. Stop saying them out loud to others and silently to yourself. With effort, you can replace these negative, destructive words with an achiever's vocabulary. Start using phrases such as, "I know I can do it," and "I will do it."

Self-talk is really a series of affirmations — positive statements said in the present tense. The effectiveness of these affirmations is determined largely by your understanding of the truth and the meaning behind the words you use.

In order for an affirmation to work, you must state it with believability.

After stating your affirmation, you must maintain an attitude that supports it, regardless of all the evidence to the contrary. Repeating an affirmation, knowing what you are saying and why you are saying it, moves your mind to a state of consciousness in which it will accept what you state as true.

Dr. Joseph Murphy, D.R.S., Ph.D., D.D., LL.D., author of *The Power of Your Subconscious Mind* says, "For an affirmation to be most effective it should be believed with all certainty that the affirmations you make are true. If you don't, your statements will be rejected by the conscious mind and the opposite will manifest."

The Power of Words

Affirmations are made up of a series of words and words are very powerful. They can create sadness, anger, and joy. So, begin paying attention to the words you use in your affirmations and in your daily dialogue — especially when the words are aimed at you. Try to eliminate all negative words from your vocabulary, particularly when you are creating affirmations that are designed to motivate.

To experience the power of words, try this experiment: Stand in front of a mirror and say to yourself: "I am a loser." Notice the response in your body. Your eyes may look toward the ground, your shoulders may slump forward, and the muscles in the body may look soft and wimpy. Now look straight into the mirror and powerfully say, "I am a winner." Look at the immediate changes in your body. You eyes become clear and focus straight ahead. Your shoulders roll back and your posture improves, and the muscles of your body firm up.

Always replace negative, self-defeating words such as:

can't	with	can or will
weak	with	strong
tired	with	energetic
unhealthy	with	healthy
never	with	possible

Using affirmations

Affirmations succeed best when they are specific and when they do not produce mental conflict. Your subconscious accepts what you really believe to be true, not just words or idle statements. Your subconscious embraces the ideas and beliefs that you embrace and works very hard to manifest them into reality. The following is a partial list of affirmations that work well for training and sports:

I am strong. I am energetic and full of vitality. I am a winner I will succeed at my goals. I enjoy my training; it makes me feel strong. It makes me feel good. I like eating nutritious food; it is healthy and satisfying. My muscles are toned. I am growing stronger every day. I feel healthy when I exercise.

Make up a list of your own affirmations which make you feel comfortable and that support your goals. Repeat them over and over. The best time for this verbal exercise is when your mind is free from distractions — right after you wake up in the morning, before you go to sleep at night, or when you are sitting quietly. During the quiet time before the games is also a prime opportunity to use affirmations.

Conclusion

Anytime you catch yourself using a word or phase that is negative and not conducive to your success, immediately stop and replace it with a new, positive word.

- Start talking to yourself positively
- Pay particular attention to the words you use in your internal and verbal dialog.
- Create affirmations that make you a winner.

34 Developing Good Relationships

If you can't get along with other people, you will dramatically narrow your chances of success.

It's estimated that 85 percent of your success in life will be determined by your social skills. This is your ability to interact positively and effectively with others to get them to cooperate with you in achieving your goals.

Learning how to develop and maintain good relationships can do more for your personal life, athletic experiences, and career perhaps than anything else.

The inability to get along with others is a primary reason for failure, frustration, and unhappiness in your life. According to one study, more than 95 percent of men and women let go from their jobs over a ten-year period were fired because of poor social skills rather than lack of competence or technical ability. According to psychologist Sydney Jourard, most of your joy in life comes from your happy relationships with other people, and most of your problems in life come from unhappy relationships. Most problems in life are the result of dealing with people.

Life is about dealing with people. Almost every situation you will encounter will involve people. The classroom, the training facility, the playing field, and the arena are great places to learn and develop communication skills.

Twelve Keys to Developing Good Relationships.

1.You must like yourself if you expect others to like you.
First and foremost you must like yourself. There is a direct link between your level of self-esteem and the health of your personality. The more you like and respect yourself, the more you will like and respect others. The more you consider yourself to be a valuable and worthwhile person the more you consider others to be valuable and worthwhile as well. The more you accept yourself as you are, the more you accept other just as they are.

2. You must learn to forgive and forget.
People make mistakes. And sometimes they say things that the don't really mean and often wish the could retract. It's your job to be forgiving. Realize that nobody is perfect, and that if someone mistreats you, is harsh, judgmental, or rude, it has nothing to do with you personally. People react and are influenced by what's going on in their lives. If someone is having a lot of stress in their life, it will more than likely show up in how they treat others. If someone mistreats you, holding a grudge is not the answer. It is a waste of time and energy. Grudges are grid-locks. They don't allow relationships to go any further. Learning to turn the other cheek and to forgive others is very important key in relationship building.

3. Open your mind to differences.
Have you ever seen anyone who was exactly like you? No two people in this world are exactly alike. Accept the fact that others are unique and appreciate their differences. Seeing things from someone else's point of view makes us think more clearly. It forces us to look at situations differently and see things in new ways. As the saying goes, "There is more than one way to skin a cat." Always work to understand and accept the other side.

4. Confront conflict and differences immediately.
Problems don't go away by avoiding them. In fact, they usually get worse. Stewing over a problem or conflict will do nothing positive for you. It drains

energy, inhibits action, and dulls performance. The way to handle conflicts and problems is to confront them head on. By facing difficulties, you are forced to work out a solution.

5. Look for the good in everyone.
Each person possesses good qualities. Judging others too quickly by their appearance, actions, and beliefs blinds you to their positive traits and talents. Before we make hasty decisions, we need to "get all the facts." Give people time to expose their true selves and avoid judging them.

6. Show interest in others.
Always talking about yourself and your interests is a good way to turn people off. The key to getting along with others is communicating, and communicating is more about listening than it is talking. Become interested in others, pay attention, and ask questions. Play like a detective, or an investigative journalist. Work at being silent when others talk. In listening to others, you can learn a lot.

7. Be upbeat and positive... Don't be a complainer.
Nobody likes a complainer. Nobody likes to hear negative, sarcastic remarks. In every situation there are two choices — to be positive or to be negative. And only you are responsible in deciding which view to take.

8. Be agreeable.
Being right all the time is not as important you might think. Other people are entitled to have their opinions and their way of doing things. This doesn't mean giving up your ideas and views. It means agreeing to accept different points of views and being willing to meet in the middle and compromise.

Have you ever noticed that nobody ever really wins an argument? When two people disagree and a compromise can't be reached then both people walk away losers.

You should always stand firm and proud of what you believe, but don't force other people to submit to your points of view. It's perfectly all right for two people who disagree to end a discussion in a stalemate. It's immature to think you have to win every situation.

By compromising, both sides come out a winner. It's a Win/Win situation.

9. Be appreciative.
People go out of their way to help you everyday. Showing your apprecia-

tion is respectful and considerate. It's been said, "Success it not a one man job." Nobody ever accomplishes anything with out the help of others. Be gracious and say, "Thank-you."

10. Give out compliments.
Everybody needs compliments. We all want positive feedback. Noticing others and complementing them appropriately is a great way to express that you care. But be careful of insincere praise. "Real" complements can always been distinguished from "fake" ones.

11. Avoid comparisons.
Making comparisons is useless. Again, no two people are the same. When we are overly concerned with where others are or with what they have, we lose perspective of your own situation. In instead of paying attention to what we can do to improve ourselves, or can accomplish, we waste timing worrying about things we have no control over. There is a saying which goes like this: "Worry about the water in your own boat." If you're so occupied with the water in the other person's boat, you won't see that the water is rising in your own.

12. Wipe out jealousy.
Jealousy is a terrible negative emotion that arises from feelings of low self-esteem and personal inadequacy. The bottom line on jealousy is that the person who is jealous really has doubts about his or her abilities and value as a person. Jealousy is a natural emotion that everybody feels. Nobody is immune to it. The green-eyed monster rears its ugly head in everyone's life from time to time. The secret in banishing it is to realize that it really has nothing to do with the other person. It all stems from your self-worth and you need to do things that make you feel worthwhile and valuable.

Conclusion
Relationships are important; throughout your life you will become involved in many of them. Learning how to communicate and get along with people will do more for your success than any other thing. To be a good athlete, student, coworker, friend, etc., it's imperative that you learn and apply each of the twelve keys to developing good relationships.

Remember, people with high levels of self-esteem can get along with almost anyone, anywhere, and in almost any situation. People with low self-esteem have difficulties getting along with others. Yet success never comes to those who go it alone. Your success depends on the cooperation and interaction of the other people in your life.

Becoming a Peak Performer

Twelve years ago when I decided to get my 250 pound overweight and out-of-shape body back into condition, I thought to myself "Wouldn't it be great to not only get into good shape, but to become one of the best displays of peak physical conditioning in the world, to reach the pinnacle of physical excellence and become one of the very best?" So I decided at that moment that I would not only get my body back into shape, but I would condition myself to reach the pinnacle of physical excellence.

As the dial stopped on the scale at the 250 pound mark, I remember looking down and saying, "Setting this goal and achieving it is going to require the performance of a life time! This is going to take maximum effort, of Olympic proportions. It's going to require, focus, intensity, sacrifice, dedication, persistence, and learning a training program that equals that of the best elite athletes of the world."

429

I knew right from the start that this goal was going to require that I become a "Peak Performer."

So I developed what I now call my "peak performance model." It has not only helped me achieve my goal of reaching the pinnacle of physical excellence, but I have been able to use it in other ways — in my career, running my own business, as well as in writing and producing books. It's a model that can be used to reach any goal you set, and it is extremely effect for training and sports.

My "Peak Performance Model"
Developing and applying the following six skills to any performance will guarantee elevating it to a higher level. Furthermore, continually applying these keys to every consecutive performance will continue to elevate your performance well into the stratosphere. Learning and applying these skills will help you become an elite peak performer.

> Skill 1. Ability to Make a Commitment
> Skill 2. Ability to Plan
> Skill 3. Ability to Focus
> Skill 4. Ability to Absorb
> Skill 5. Ability to Reflect
> Skill 6. Ability to Redirect

Let me explain to you how this works.

The first thing I had to do to get my body in to peak condition was to **commit** 100% to that goal. That meant dedicating time, energy, effort, and a financial investment. Without a 100% commitment, it's easy to quit when the going gets tough and obstacles threaten your success. Committing also means getting away from people and activities that don't support your best interests. It means saying goodbye to some old friends and making room for new ones that will share and support the success of your goals. It means reestablishing your priorities and eliminating activities from your schedule that may interfere with your progress.

Without a **plan**, you can't accomplish anything. It's like getting behind the wheel of a car without a destination in mind. You end up nowhere. Developing a plan is really the same thing as having a guide. It will show you what needs to be done and how to do it. I had to develop a plan to follow to get into great shape. That plan became my daily guide or training program.

It's impossible to be in two places at the same time. A wandering mind never accomplishes anything. Developing the skill to be able to **focus** on what you are doing when you are doing it is the way you get maximum performance. In other words when you're training, your mind should be in the same room with you.

When I was first starting to exercise to get back into shape, my mind would often wander and I would lose focus on what I was doing. The end result was that my training sessions were not productive. But with effort, I was able to develop my concentration skills to the point where they are as effective as harnessing the power of sunlight through a magnifying glass to burn a leaf.

Absorbing or connecting to your performance is the way you get into what is called the "zone." This is that place that peak performers slip into when they are totally connected to what they are doing. It's when effort become effortless, and performance is perfect. It's when all the balls you throw magically go through the hoop.

The ability to absorb and connect is only developed through hours and hours of practice and repetition.

Good performances as well as bad performances are valuable to the peak performer. Developing the skill to **reflect** over our performances, both good and bad is the way you improve. My bad training taught me how to make the necessary adjustments that made me successful. They showed me what works and what doesn't.

Reflecting is sort of like watching and reviewing the tapes of your performance. When I played football in college, every move that I made on the field was captured on video. After practice I reviewed the tapes, learning from both the good and bad moves I had made.

Developing the skill of mentally video taping your performances or practices will give you all the information you will need to make improvements as long as you have the ability to **redirect**.

Redirecting is simply the skill of taking lessons learned in previous experiences and applying them to the next performance. Mentally reflecting over my training sessions always gave me valuable feedback, but the feedback was of no value until it was put to use. Taking the valuable feedback gained from reflecting and redirecting will make your future performances more successful.

Conclusion

- ◆ Becoming great at anything will require maximum performance, whether your goal is to become an elite doctor, athlete, student, performer, musician, etc.
- ◆ Knowledge is useless without action. In other words knowing how to do something means nothing until you develop the ability do it.
- ◆ All success on the playing field, and in life, is dependent on one thing — your ability to perform.

Success is related to performance. Apply these keys and become a "peak performer for life!"

36

Attitude is Everything

When I played football in college we had a quarterback on the team that was very good. He was so good that he would have probably received many awards at the end of the season. Then one day before practice our head coach gathered us together and told us he had kicked the quarterback off the team. We were all devastated. Everyone knows that the quarterback is the engine of the team. And teams are always looking for good quarterbacks, especially with the talents of the one we had.

Our coach went on to explain the circumstances of his dismissal; it seems that the quarterback had a lousy attitude. Although he was very talented, he didn't feel like he should have to work so hard in practice or follow the same rules everybody else did. His attitude was very negative, gray, and dismal.

Our coach was wise. He knew no matter how much talent and ability someone has, it can't compensate for a bad attitude. And even worse, a bad attitude is contagious. It affects everyone around it.

I'm sure the coach lost some sleep over making this decision. He was taking a real risk. If the team didn't win, he could lose his job. Without one of the best players, in the most key position, he was really stacking the cards against himself. But he made the decision for the long-term good of the team. Although we did not win the conference that year, I think we all received a much more valuable lesson. Our coach made the right decision for the right reason. A bad attitude is the worst crippling performance disease one can have. Nobody wins with a bad attitude.

A Good Attitude

There is one thing in common that all great achievers have — a good attitude. This will do more for a person than talent and skill.

Your attitude will always be the determining factor in the success and failures in your life. As an athlete, a great attitude can overcompensate for lack of talents, abilities, physical deficiencies, and skills.

What is Attitude

Your attitude is the way you approach life; it is your angle of attack. It is your general mental tone and outward expression of your inner thoughts and feelings. A positive attitude is generally optimistic and cheerful. A negative attitude is usually pessimistic, gloomy, and unhappy.

Your attitude is one of the best indicators of the person you really are deep inside. It's the way you tell the world who you really are. And people usually reflect back to you your attitude towards them.

Your inborn attributes, your natural talents and abilities, and the inner aspects of your personality are largely fixed at birth. They are your genetic heritage. It's not easy to change them.

Your acquired attributes are the skills and abilities you develop by channeling your natural talents through your education and experience.

You can develop, improve, and change your acquired attributes over time through study and practice. But the process is slow and deliberate, requiring patience, discipline, and considerable effort.

The key to this development and improvement is your attitude.

Since the quality of your attitude can be improved almost with out limit, even a person with average inborn attributes and average acquired attributes can perform at a high level if he or she has a very positive mental attitude. Your attitude can be improved immediately and almost without limit. That's why your attitude is the key determines of what and how much your accomplish.

Your attitude is under direct control of your will. You can decide what it is going to be every minute of every day.

Your attitude comes from your expectations. Your expectations about yourself and your life greatly influence your personality.

If you expect good things to happen, are positive, optimistic, and see the good in people and situations, then you have a good attitude. If you are negative, pessimistic, and see the bad in others and situations, you have a negative attitude.

Positive expectations are the mark of a good attitude, and go hand in hand with happiness, fulfillment, and self-confidence. Good attitudes give you sort of a mental resilience that enables you to respond to challenges you face

Bad attitude is flu-like; it has a way of putting a dark cloud over everything you do.

Developing a positive attitude is the necessary step to unlocking your full potential. I have never seen anyone accomplish great things with a bad attitude. A bad attitude strips you of ambition, robs you of accomplishments, drains your energy, and causes people to think negatively about you.

A good test of your attitude is how you react when things go wrong. I believe that attitude is 90% of the key to all success, whether it's in sports, the classroom, or the gym.

A Good Attitude is Up to Your "Self"
It is dependent on individual levels of:

- Self-respect — Our feelings about ourselves, reflected in how we treat ourselves.
- Self-responsibility — Taking responsibility for our actions gives us responsibility over our lives.
- Self-discipline — Our behavior that results from our individualized methods and rules.

- Self-image — The image you have of yourself.
- Self-esteem — Confidence and respect for yourself.
- Self- direction — Our paths, the course of action we set for ourselves.
- Self-pride — Proper respect for your own dignity and worth.
- Self-belief — Trust and confidence in who we are and what we believe in.
- Self-confidence — Inner trusting of our abilities, desires, wishes, and actions.
- Self-motivation — Reason and desire behind our actions.

Things that Threaten a Good Attitude

A good attitude can be deflated by many things, such as:

- criticism
- lack of motivation
- lack of dedication
- unwillingness to accept responsibility
- lack of goals
- fear
- fatigue
- lack of skill
- not enough practice
- losing
- negative people

Everyone Cops a Bad Attitude at Sometime

A bad attitude is sort of like a cold; everybody eventually catches it. It can start out just mildly annoying, with only a few sniffles here and there. But if left unchecked, a cold could easily turn into a full-blown case of the flu, and you'll find yourself flat on your back and in bed for a week.

The trick to halting a bad attitude is detecting those first negative thoughts and replacing them with productive thoughts. This will help you break through those dark clouds. Remember, everybody has gets a bad attitude from time to time, so don't sweat it when it happens to you.

Let it pass, don't worry about it. If you are truly on course, you will get through it; if you don't, it is time to reassess your priorities and give yourself an attitude adjustment.

Conclusion

The key to having a great attitude is to focus on the positive, the things you can control. Keep your attention on the things necessary to make the most of your natural abilities. Through personal experience, I have always found that you win ball games, make the grades, close sales, and succeed in business by having a great attitude!

37 Confidence

Confidence is critical for success in training, sports, and in life. Without confidence, you can't step up to the plate, attempt the record life, apply for the dream job, or even get behind the wheel of a car. It is the fuel that drives all great accomplishments.

My definition of confidence is: a complete belief in your ability and total self-assurance that you can reach the goals that are important to you. Confidence is how strongly you believe in your ability to reach your destination.

We gain confidence from:

♦ Preparation
♦ Practice
♦ Pressure

Complete preparation — planning our training, doing all the homework. This enables us to take action. There is an amazing power that each of us possesses when we get to the point where we can

say, "I have done all my homework. I've made my plan. I am ready."

Preparation also builds the endurance needed to keep pushing on when things become challenging and obstacles threaten our progress.

Practice — is the time we learn and master the skills we need to have in order to reach our goals. High achievement always follows the mastering of skills — learning techniques, gaining knowledge, and improving our abilities. Practice allows our confidence to grow and helps us develop discipline.

Pressure — Although many believe that pressure is bad, it is really very good for us. Pressure or stress keeps us on our goals. It propels us into action. It provides us with motivation to perform. Being able to handle pressure does a lot for our confidence. Maintaining composure, staying focused, and persevering during high pressure situations thickens our skin to life's inevitable stumbling blocks. Soon we are able to tolerate more and more stress, which builds our confidence levels even higher and higher.

Confidence is generated from poise. And poise is not something you pursue — it is something you embody. True poise is simply being yourself and not wearing a fake mask projecting what we think others want us to be. Confidence comes from doing what you do in relationship to who you are and developing your own unique strengths and abilities.

Confidence is critical to the peak performer's psychological makeup. Confident people are able to "let go and make things happen." If your goal is to be a peak performer, then spend time building your confidence.

Setting Goals

All dreams and accomplishments begin with a vision. From the vision, you build a plan, you develop a road map. You set goals to work toward.

The process described in this chapter are just the basics for achieving your dreams, for reaching your goals.

How to Identify Your Goals

To set goals, you must first find out what is really important to you. No one else can set goals for you. A goal is something you must believe in, and you must be willing to work for. A goal is something that has meaning and worth for you.

I use these questions to help people identify their goals:

- What is the most important thing in your life right now?
- Is there more than one thing important to you?
- What is the one thing you dream about doing?

Rules for Goal Setting
The goals you set must:

♦ Be yours
♦ Harmonize with your life
♦ Challenge you and offer a positive reward
♦ Be positive and organized, focused and purposeful

Setting goals helps us define who we are and who we are becoming. They create positive pressure to keep us from becoming bored with life. They help us clarify our direction and help us make important decisions. Goals keep us moving forward and funnel our energies in positive outlets.

As you work toward goals, you will find that your self-esteem is enhanced and you will come to like yourself more. This in turn gives you the confidence to set and achieve more goals.

Short-term & Long-term Goals
You should always set short-term and long-term goals. A short-term goal may be to go through the next 24 hours and eat only healthy foods or to keep your thoughts positive. Another short-term goal may be to finish the term paper before the end of the weekend.

Long-term goals may be fitness levels that you want to achieve a year from now, or the number of college applications you want to submit before the end of the semester. You can even set long-term career goals to aim for upon completion of college.

Nine Step Action Plan for Setting and Achieving Goals
1. Open your mind to all possibilities.
2. Write them down.
3. List the benefits and rewards of achieving this goal.
4. Analyze your position and starting point.
5. Set a deadline.
6. List the obstacles that stand in your way.
7. Identify any additional information or skill that you may need to develop to reach these goals.
8. Make a list of the people who can help you achieve these goals.
9. Be willing to revise your goals.

Using visualization techniques described in Chapter 41 will help you reach your goals. If any goal is to be achieved, you must first see in and feel it. You must also be willing to reshape or redefine your goals.

Changing your mind or your direction is perfectly acceptable. Sometimes we set goals for ourselves based on the expectations of other people in our lives.

Conclusion

♦ Don't let goal setting intimidate you. It's not as hard as it sounds.
♦ Only reach for those goals that are important to you.
♦ See yourself in your mind's eye achieving your dreams.

Developing Mental
Toughness

For the longest time I thought mental toughness was something you were born with — you either had it or didn't have it. It wasn't until I really started studying how the mind works did I discover that it is possible to develop mental toughness.

In the book *The Einstein Factor*, authors Win Wenger, Ph.D. and Richard Poe state that new research suggests that the superior achievements of famous thinkers may have been more the result of mental conditioning than genetic superiority. They claim one can learn to condition the mind to achieve greater levels of sharpness, insight, and overall intelligence.

It appears that our minds can be developed, strengthened, and become more powerful if we learn to train them like we train our bodies. Lifting weights stresses our muscles and forces them to grow and get stronger and more powerful. Exposing our minds to challenges, new experiences, and goals stresses our minds in a good way, forcing our minds to become stronger and more powerful.

According to Sports Psychologist Jim Loehr, author of the book *Toughness Training For Life*, mental stress is good for you. "Exposure to the right stress trains you to face your fears and continue the fight."

Mental toughness is important in sports, You'll need it when the scoreboard has you down 20 to 3. Mental toughness is also important in life. You'll need it when your company eliminates your position and lays you off.

Great Ways to Build Your Mental Toughness
I have found some keys to developing mental toughness:

Be willing be first.
Step out in front of the line. Be willing to take risks in front of others.

Accept challenges.
Facing challenges does something magical to us. Whether you succeed or not is not important. What is important is the effort. The struggle makes us grow.

Try new things.
New experiences teach us a lot. If you stay in one place, you will grow weeds. Vow to be adventurous. Try a new food; bike or roller blade in an area different than the one you're used to; watch an educational program instead of a sitcom.

Face your weaknesses.
One of the reasons I started writing books was because writing was a weakness for me. When I wrote my first book, it was like climbing Mt. Everest. I would spend hours and days at the keyboard. But nothing I wrote seemed to make sense. But by sticking with it, continually facing what was once a weakness I was able to turn it into a strength. There is a saying: "Face a weakness and soon it will become a strength."

Welcome problems, set backs, crisis as part of the process.
Problems are good for us: they are character-building and enriching. They offer opportunities for self-awareness and change. Problems and conflicts make us stronger.

Strengthen your body.
It's simple: a strong body equals a strong mind. Make physical training a lifelong commitment. Continue to lift weights. Weight training does some things to us that science can't explain. It gives us a feeling of mental power

and the extra edge to face challenges and obstacles. I always train extra hard with weights when I am writing and producing books because it's so challenging. Everyday something pops up threatening the completion of the project. I know that a good weight training session give me the extra edge to go back into the office and face the challenges head on.

Train your brain.
Learning is great mental exercise. The best exercise for the brain is reading. Strive to learn as much as you can. Set up a library. Read articles and books on subjects such as self-development, peak performance, and anything else that even mildly peaks your interest.

Get your cardiovascular system in shape.
Having a strong heart and lungs will give you extra power to break through obstacles as well as the endurance to ride the waves of adversity. Work at keeping your cardiovascular system in shape. Get in those three, 30-minute aerobic training sessions each week.

Push your limits.
Complacency is what really killed the cat, not curiosity. Once you've attained a goal you set for yourself, set another one. Without goals to strive for, life can become very boring.

Get plenty of rest.
As Vince Lombardi said, "Fatigue makes cowards of us all." It's hard to be mentally resilient when your running at half speed. A big part of mental toughness is having energy. We all know how hard it is to make any effort to do anything when we are tired. Sleep, rest, and relaxation are necessary to recharge our batteries.

Practice good nutritional habits.
Feeding our bodies is obviously important. We have spent a lot of time talking bout how foods effect your body and performance. But the foods you eat also fuel your brain and affect your mental sharpness and ability to think with a clear, focused mind. Pay particular attention to how the foods you eat make you feel mentally.

Conclusion

Perseverance is the basis for building mental toughness. Taking the easy route and shying away from challenges will make your mind soft and weak. By training your mind and body for toughness, you can rise to any challenge and be able to handle the pressures that go along with life's stresses. I hope I have made this clear throughout this book: you are a marvelous creation, loaded with awesome potential. The things that will hold you back — negative beliefs, laziness, and complacency — will appear from time to time and challenge you. When this happens make an extra effort to spend some time working on your mental toughness!

40 Mentors & Modeling

Kris with three-time Mr. Olympia Frank Zane.

One of the biggest success secrets that I have ever seen lies in the use of mentors and modeling. For just about every goal there is someone has had the same goal or similar goal and has succeeded at it. When I was in high school, my goal was to play college football. An older guy that had graduated several years ahead of me was playing college football. In the summers he would come home to work and train in the same gym that I did. I can remember making it a point to schedule my training at the same time he did so I could be in the gym to watch him train and learn his exercise techniques. Also, I would strike up conversations, telling him of my goals and asking him advice. During those summers I learned a tremendous amount; I watched every move he made; I modeled my training after his; I ate the same foods; I ran the same distances; I even worked the same summer job!

And guess what? I later when on to play college football because of those valuable tips and lessons I learned by modeling my training program after his. He was a great guy, from a good family, and he treated me with kindness and respect. He was always willing to give me advice.

Although I didn't know it at the time, I had chosen a mentor and modeled a successful path toward my goal. I had chosen to seek the advice and counseling of someone who had "been there, done that." Who knows what might have happened had I not done that? I probably would have struggled and failed many times over before reaching my goals.

Mentoring and modeling are important because they:

♦ Show us that our goals can be achieved
♦ Show us ways to achieve our goals
♦ Shortcut the process/save us time
♦ Motivate us
♦ Guide and coach us
♦ Offer support

Mentoring

I like to define mentoring as the act of seeking advice and guidance from someone you respect and look up to, a person who is "experience rich" and possesses much wisdom. A good mentor is someone who leads by example, who walks the talk, and conducts themselves in a respectful manner.

Mentors can show us how things are done by:

♦ Taking special interest in us
♦ Providing encouragement
♦ Offering valuable advice

Mentors are all around you. Some of them you may know personally, some you can read about in book. Reading about people who have accomplished great things is a good way to find a mentor even though you don't meet them, talk with them, or ask them directly for advice. The shelves in book stores are filled with books written by people who have succeeded. You can get success lessons from athletes, business persons, doctors, lawyers, and many others. Just about anything you have an interest in learning more about and accomplishing in life has already been experienced by someone who has taken the time to share their success secrets by writing a book.

Modeling

Most challenging goals have been accomplished before. When I was training back in high school, I used my mentor's training schedule and routine as a model to set up my own program. I did not copy it exactly, but I used the basic structure and added my own little twists to fit my individual needs. I modeled my training and approach after someone who had devised a system that was successful.

Modeling doesn't mean becoming a carbon copy of someone else. After all a copy is a fake. That's not the goal. You still have to be yourself; you still have to include your own individual exercises and routines in your training program. In modeling the approach, you take the basics, sort through what's relevant to your needs, and apply these to your individual goals and ambitions.

Play like a detective. Ask: what the person did; how they trained; the problems they ran into, etc. You're looking for their system. Once you figure it out, you can use it to pattern and construct your own system.

Set Up a Round Table of Advisors

For many of our goals, getting the advice from several people is a better more complete way to learn. It's been said that success is seldom a one person job. I have found a great way of learning is to set up a round table of advisors. You put together a group of individuals who are extremely talented and knowledgeable in areas that coincide with your goals. Companies do this all the time; they set up boards of directors — advisory personnel, whose roles are to advise and supervise the affairs of the institution or corporation.

Succeeding with most goals requires special knowledge and training in many areas. For instance, even though I was modeling the approach of someone who was playing college football, I knew that it was going to take more than a good physical training program to get me into college. There were academic requirements and entrance exams to pass. There were also financial expenses and housing logistics to workout.

So I sought the advice of experts in these individual areas. I got an academic advisor to help me prepare for the entrance exams. I talked with a financial strategist. And I obtained information on housing from students presently at the university.

These people all became my round table of advisors. Again, the goal was to play college football. But in order to accomplish this, it took more than having a mentor and a good training program. It took expert advice and counsel from many people to help me reach and accomplish my goal. I highly recommend that you follow this approach. Set up your own round table of advisors.

Conclusion

Remember, if someone else has done it before, so can you. If not, you can be the first. Then you can be somebody else's mentor.

- ♦ Choosing a mentor is not about joining a fan club; it's simply selecting a guide, leader, or main advisor to help you reach your goals.
- ♦ Modeling a successful approach is a great way to set up your own success system. Getting advice from experts in their own specialities is the best possible way to get the very best advice and guidance you can.

41 Seeing is Achieving

Lie on the couch and close your eyes. Relax... Get yourself into a state of relaxation where you have no immediate concerns. Let all the tension of the day leave your body.

Your about to run the final heat of the 100-meter dash at the high school state finals. As you walk up to your starting block, you gaze to the left seeing four opponents next to you bending down and getting set in their lanes. A quick turn of the head, and you see the three opponents on your right also getting into their lanes. There are eight of you, and you are in the fifth lane just a little outside of the center of the track. It's a wonderful sunny Saturday afternoon in June. It's warm. As the sun beats down on your shoulders, you can feel the warmth throughout your body. You can smell the aroma of fresh cut grass hanging in the air throughout the stadium. You're anxiously awaiting the sound of the starting gun, coiled in your stance and ready to spring forward like a tiger on the prowl. You hear the gun go off, and you shoot like a rocket out in front of the pack. You're in the lead with just two meters to go. You can see the finish line rapidly approaching. The taste of victory is in your mouth. As you lean forward, you can feel the tape stretch and break across your chest.

Congratulations, you won the race! You're the champion! The view is wonderful as you look out over the admiring crowd. You look like a champion on top of the podium as you bow forward and the official hangs the gold medal around your neck.

Using Your Imagination

What you have just done in the exercise above is what is called visualization. If you have been involved in training or sports, then you probably have heard the term. Although it sounds like "weird science," visualization is really something easy to do. It is no more than using your imagination to see yourself accomplish something before you actually do it. We all visualize many different things in the course of the day — where we are going to sit on the bus, who we are going to ask to the dance, scoring the winning touchdown in Friday night's ball game, and much, much more. Everyone has the ability to visualize by using their imagination.

Visualization for Training and Sports

Visualization is extremely effective in training, sports, and performance. In high school, I used to visualize myself playing for a university. I could see myself wearing the uniform, playing in the stadium.

I have also used it extensively to get my 250 pound overweight and out-of-shape body into peak physical condition. As I was exercising the pounds off, I would use my imagination to plant images of my body being in fantastic shape.

Visualization works so well because vision is our predominate sense. What we "see" we tend to believe is "real". Visualization changes beliefs into reality. For it to be most effective, it should involve all five senses: sight , sound, taste, feel, and smell. That's what we did in the exercise above.

Research shows that high achiever's are able to visualize their goals clearly. Successful people are motivated by vivid and precise mental images of what they want to achieve. When you hold a picture long enough in your mind, the enormous power of the mind will become set on achieving it until it becomes a reality.

To effectively visualize you should:
♦ Be relaxed, with a clear, calm mind.
♦ Pick one goal to focus on.
♦ Let your mind run freely, imagining all the ways to reach that goal.
♦ Use all five senses in your visualization.
♦ Rehearse your images at least 2-3 times a day.

Conclusion
♦ Use visualization as a tool to boost your training, super charge your athletic performances, reach challenging, personal goals, and succeed in all areas of your life.
♦ Ask yourself: "Am I taking time to visualize what I want?" "Do I see myself as a winner, a success, a peak performer?" "Are my images clear and vivid?" "Do I really believe what I am seeing?"
♦ Let your imagination run wild and remember to see, heart, taste, smell, and see your success.

42 Really Good Advice for Parents

This is a book I really feel good about writing. When I was a teenager I was fortunate enough to get involved in sports and weight training. Today, when I look back, I can't even begin to believe just how much those early experiences have positively impacted my life. It's been twenty years since I picked up my first dumbbell. Because of that my life has been blessed with many wonderful experiences, and most importantly my health is A+. Writing and producing books is hard work. Although it is tedious, time consuming, and difficult, the end result offers me an outlet to share these wonderful life-changing practices and principles.

That's why I worked so hard to write and produce this book. If this message can reach one young person and impact their life, as it has mine, then the time, effort, money, and resources spent will be well worth it.

Whenever I talk to a teenager or young person, I always tell them that the lessons of success in life are taught on the playing field and in the gym. Hard work, commitment, persistence, dedication, positive attitude, sacrifice, and sweat have always been and will always be he prerequisites of success.

As the father of three wonderful children, I'm sure we share the same concerns:

We want our children to be mentally and physically healthy. We also want to see them excel, have self-confidence, develop good self-esteem and a positive attitude. We also hope that they have the ability to set and pursue worthy goals, be industrious, ambitious, and also live prosperous meaningful lives.

Plain and simple, we want the best for our kids.

One of the most frequently asked questions that I receive from parents expressing concerns about their son or daughter is: "How can I get them involved in health and fitness?"

Parents' Roles in Their Teenagers' Health

My answer to parents is not one that is always well received. The best way to influence your teenager to live healthy, exercise, and eat right is to set an example. Teenagers become their environment. You are a role model for your child or children. Your actions, activities, and beliefs will become theirs. So the very best thing you can do to support and influence your child to live a healthy lifestyle is to live one yourself. After all what sense does it make for a parent to scold a child on the negatives of smoking, as they puff always on a cigarette? Or to tell a child they need to exercise when they're getting a little soft around the belly?

My wife and I own a hair salon. Every once in awhile she comes to me frustrated about the employees at the shop. Most recently she came to me expressing concern about the way the employees were dressing at work. She felt that their dress had become sloppy, and felt like the employees were not representing themselves, nor the business, in a professional manner. And I agreed; I had thought that we needed to make some changes for awhile.

She asked, "Should we have a meeting, or maybe outline a dress code? What should we do?" I immediately told her to get in the car. She asked where we were going. I said, "To buy you some new clothes." I explained to her that the way you influence and lead people is to serve as an example.

"If you want the employees to dress more professionally in your business then you, as the owner, the leader, need to do so also." She bought the new clothes, wore them to work, and soon the problem fixed itself.

If your children are continually exposed to the positives of health, exercise, and eating right by you, eventually they will more than likely follow your example — most of the time. There may be times, however, when no matter what you do, your child will go his or her own way. And that's okay, because you have done the best you can by setting an example for your child. Remember: ultimately, everyone is responsible for their own actions — even your children.

What works — What doesn't work

I had a client who became very concerned over her teenage daughter's health. At age 14, she weighed about 185 pounds. It had become quite an issue around the house as well as became a problem at school because some of her classmates were beginning to tease her.

My client informed me that she was going to force her daughter to start exercising, everyday. She set up a walking routine and was scheduling weekly weigh-ins, as well as monitoring every morsel that went into her daughter's mouth. There were also guidelines and restrictions placed upon the daughter's time, as well as consequences administered if she did not lose weight consistently from week to week. My client was fed up, and she was determined to make her daughter lose the weight.

Then one day my client asked for my advice. I told my client that her plan was going to end in a disaster! I was quite frank. I said, "Look, you're 30 pounds overweight. What happens if I give you the same guidelines? What happens if I force you to exercise, weigh you in, watch every morsel that goes into your mouth? You would hate me in a week." But my client disagreed; she assured me that she knew her daughter and that this was the only way to make her lose weight.

The daughter was humiliated; it crushed her self-esteem, and she now hates anything to do with exercise, eating right, and is gaining more weight every day. You simple can't force a teenager, or anyone else, to exercise and eat right. The only thing you can do is set the example by living a health and fitness lifestyle.

What's Worked for Me

I know firsthand how this approach works. Recently, my wife said, "Can you believe just how much Kraig has changed this year? He is exercising on his own, eating healthy foods, slimmed down, and now supports an athletic slender build. Just a year ago, he was a pudgy energyless kid, who couldn't get off the couch, lived on chips, and thought exercise was a curse."

We never forced or coerced him to eat what we were eating. We never told him that he should exercise or play sports. We simply lived a healthy lifestyle and let him see the benefits for himself. It was his decision to begin exercising and eating right. Even today, our role as parents is still just to lead by example.

Some Do's and Don'ts

Do not:
 force, coerce, give ultimatums, scold, ridicule, or tease

Never put your child in embarrassing situations, especially when it comes to his or her physical appearance. Never joke about them being overweight, or bargain with them to lose weight. We all know what it's like when loved ones tell us something that we don't like or want to hear. We get resentful. That's what will happen to a teenager, and if not handled delicately, the damage can be irreparable.

All these things damage their self-esteem and will build walls between you and your child, at a time when communication and support is essential for their well-being.

Do:
 encourage, support, and set a good example

Sports is not just about winning; fitness is not just about getting an hourglass figure or fitting into size four jeans. Sports, fitness, and training is a time of discovery. These are activities that help people of all ages learn about themselves and build character, especially our young people. A child should be encouraged to engage in these activities with the goal being self-development, to become a better person and develop skills to become more healthy and enhance one's life.

Final Reminders

- ◆ Make health and fitness part of your lifestyle and more than likely your children will adopt healthy habits when they are ready.
- ◆ That's my best advice, as a parent. I hope it works for you as well as it has for me.

Closing Thoughts

43

hope you have enjoyed the book. There is a tremendous amount of information in these pages. I set the book up in mini sections that are easily assessable, so you can reference the material whenever you need it. At any time you can quickly, look to the table of contents, turn to the section of interest, and get the information you want without having to read through pages and pages of text.

There is so much information in the book that it is impossible to grasp it in one reading. I encourage you to come back to this book as much as you like: for training tips, nutritional information, or when seeking the mental edge.

Training the Teenager for the Game of Their Life does an excellent job of making the parallel between fitness, training, sports, and future success in life. Everything affects everything; what you do today will affect what happens tomorrow. What you do in the classroom will affect how you play on the field, and how you play on the field will affect how you do in the classroom. Those extra sprints you ran last week will show up some day, maybe in a job interview, or when you're in line for a job promotion.

Keep this in mind, as you go through the next phase of your life training and you continue participating in sports. When those sprints get tough, they are going to payoff "big time" someday down the road. Those bench presses and crunches that you are grueling through will one day make you a bank president or the number one salesman in your company. Because "everything affects everything."

With the information in this book you can become a winner in every area of your life. By using the tips and techniques outlined in this book, I have seen people:

- ♦ Earn college scholarships
- ♦ Land dream jobs
- ♦ Become millionaires
- ♦ Start their own businesses
- ♦ Become professional athletes
- ♦ Become celebrities
- ♦ Get into fantastic shape
- ♦ Get elected to office

The "Real" Rewards of Training and Sports

Whenever I am interviewed, or talk to a group, I always make this statement: "Everything that I ever needed to know about succeeding in life, I learned in the gym and on the playing field." This statement simply means that the lessons gained from training and sports are the same lessons that you need to learn in order to become a success at anything. These valuable lessons teach us many important things like, how to:

- ♦ Be committed
- ♦ Have determination
- ♦ Build our confidence
- ♦ Develop our dreams
- ♦ Set and achieve goals
- ♦ Be dedicated
- ♦ Have the willingness to do the work
- ♦ Practice
- ♦ Develop the ability to delay gratification
- ♦ Take risks

- Face our fears
- Make sacrifices
- Learn preparedness
- Learn from failure and success

I always tell people that the goal for training and participating in sports should be focused on long-term personal development more so than on the immediate results. It's not just winning the game, championship, or contest, or developing huge biceps, or a beautiful body, or getting in shape for bikini season that matters.

Training and sports parallel character completion. If you train or participate with the ultimate goal of becoming a more well-rounded person — a better student, athlete, family member, or citizen, then you will have tapped into the life-enhancing lessons that these activities teach us.

Remember this!

Great accomplishments are the result of activity and action. Even what may seem like the smallest thing that may have little effect on your life can eventually snowball into a major driving force down the road. Two pushups today will become four tomorrow; four tomorrow will become six the next day and so on.

At this stage in your life you will never have a better time to start planing your future and controlling your destiny. Be prepared to take some bold steps. Work at generating clear plans and always remember that you are the captain of your own ship.

Taking bold steps means doing new things, going to new places, meeting new and different people. It also means taking new risks, meeting new challenges, facing your fears. Remember as you look at these last pictures always face your weaknesses. By doing so they will become new strengths.

Never, and I repeat never, be afraid to make mistakes or to fail at something. It's okay to lose; it's part of the process of becoming excellent. I think back to all the mistakes I have made over the years in my training and now I realize that they were necessary. It's how I got to where I am. Mistakes and failures teach us when and how to make adjustments and change directions. They are teachers. Welcome them into your life.

The goal for you should be to strive for personal excellence. Notice I did not say perfection. Perfection is not a state that exists in human achievement.

Life will never be perfect , but it can be excellent!

My Wish for You

My wish in writing this book is that it will serve you now and throughout the rest of your life. If you apply the principles and skills of these 43 chapters, I know you will meet with success on the playing field, in personal relationships, and in your career. BUT it means you must adopt and practice these skills; commit to living and breathing them. If you don't, this will simply wind up being only an enjoyable reading experience.

With the information in this book you can go out and become a WINNER IN LIFE!

Also by Kris Gebhardt

Available in bookstores nationwide or order direct by calling 1-800-643-2412.

Featuring

PERSONAL TRAINING SYSTEM™

"The Professional Series P.T.S. is the most innovative training system available."

**For
Information
Please
Call
1-800-643-2412**